START YOUR NOTARY PUBLIC & LOAN SIGNING AGENT BUSINESS

THE INSIDERS GUIDE TO STARTING A SIX-FIGURE NOTARY SIDE HUSTLE (ALL STATE REQUIREMENTS INCLUDED)

LSAUSA EDUCATION

CONTENTS

Introduction   vii

1. What is a Notary?   1
2. Why Become a Notary Public or Loan
   Signing Agent?   10
3. What is Required – And How Much
   Does it Cost?   23
4. Becoming Certified as a Notary Public
   or Loan Signing Agent (State-by-State)   44
5. Working as a Notary (State-By-State
   Requirements, Terms, and Authorized
   Duties)   58
6. Getting Your First Clients & Marketing
   Your Business   95
7. Loan Signing Agent Masterclass   105
8. Becoming a Remote Online Notary &
   Further Income Generating Activities   119
9. Notary Business Expansion Strategies   141
10. Permit Renewals, FAQs, Taking
    Payments & More   145

Conclusion   153

COPYRIGHT & DISCLAIMER

By reading this document, the reader agrees that under no circumstances is the author or publisher responsible for any losses, direct or indirect, which are incurred as a result of the use of the information contained within this document, including, but not limited to, — errors, omissions, or inaccuracies.

Book Cover Icon License: **Freepik Subscription** *56ebd41d-19d4-444c-a966-d86168186415*

Copyright Registration #: Contact the Publisher

INTRODUCTION

"Each and every notary public has a crucial role in combating identity theft. Notaries serve as our front line of defense, and the public is safer because of the job they do."

- Ken Salazar

~

Are you looking for a way to earn extra income? Perhaps you're interested in starting your own business? Or are you tired of working a 9-to-5 job and want more control over your career?

You're organized and detail-oriented, and you've been told that you have excellent communication skills and the resolve to stay calm under pressure. If only there were a job opportunity that allowed you to capitalize on your talents..

Your mind flashes back to when you paid a notary to witness your signature. You wondered how that person had become a notary and why they were allowed to charge money to watch you sign some documents.

This leads you to another memory – a conversation you overheard in the lunchroom at work. A colleague bragged about his side-gig and claimed to be putting his son through college by witnessing documents for a few hours a week. He referred to himself as an "impartial witness" and a "state officer" and boasted about being an important part of the legal system.

A little online research shows that notaries and loan signing agents are in high demand. You learn that most of the work of a notary is straightforward – witnessing signatures and verifying identities – but that sometimes they're tasked with a more complicated task like notarizing estate planning paperwork.

Maybe you read some personal accounts online and found that becoming a notary can be challenging, but the consensus is that it's worth the effort. Notaries seem proud of their role and opportunity to make a difference in their community. Of course, the extra income and the convenience of working just a few hours here and there are distinct bonuses too.

Notaries are highly trusted individuals who are responsible for witnessing signatures on important documents, ensuring that the signer is actually who they say they are and that they understand the document they are signing. As a notary, you are expected to maintain the highest standards of professionalism and integrity. In return, you will find that being a notary is a rewarding and fulfilling experience.

In the United States, as of 2023, there are currently more than **4.5 million notary publics**, with a proportion of these notaries also qualified loan signing agents. The notary industry is largely untapped, with significant potential for growth. For individuals looking for a side hustle, notary work can be an excellent option.

Notaries can choose to work in their local community or remotely and don't need to be available during traditional business hours. It is this flexibility and autonomy that leads many people towards becoming a notary.

The fees associated with notarizing documents can vary depending on several factors, including where you live. Most notaries charge by the document, with simple documents such as affidavits bringing in between $10 and $25 each. The rate increases for complex signings like trusts. A loan signing agent can easily charge more than $200 for a mortgage document.

Service add-ons can also affect the price, with notaries who offer mobile services typically charging more than those working in an office setting. Notaries may charge extra for *rush services* or for notarizing multiple documents at once. As a notary or loan signing agent, you would only need to service a handful of clients to bring in $1,000 per week comfortably.

The cost of becoming a notary also varies, with some states requiring notaries to purchase a surety bond and others charging a notary fee. Overall, the startup costs associated with becoming a notary are relatively low compared to other business ventures and side-gigs.

If you're interested in learning more about being a notary (whether you're still in the information-gathering stage or you're ready to start your own notary business), this is the book for you. You'll have access to valuable information on what the job entails, how much you can earn, what kind of training and education you'll need, and the practical aspects of setting up your notary business, no matter which state you live in.

What sets this book apart from the others on the market is the unfiltered access you'll have to my experience as a successful notary business owner. Not only will this book educate and inform you, but it will also motivate you to take the necessary steps to start your notary side hustle or business. This book is a must-read whether you want supplemental income or a full-time notary business.

At this point, you may be wondering who I am and why I'm in the position to advise you on starting your own notary business. My name is Fred Becker, and I'm a practicing notary and loan signing agent. Now the time has finally come to write my first book on the subject. Since 2009 I have owned and run a successful notary business. Two years after qualifying as a notary, I became a loan signing agent. I've performed tens of thousands of notarizations for clients throughout the United States. I'm a member of both the National Notary Association and the American Society of Notaries. Now, in this book, I'm sharing everything I know so that you can benefit from my knowledge and experience.

There's never been a better time to get into the notary business. The market is growing rapidly. As our population grows, the demand for notaries continues to increase. Every day, millions of documents need to be notarized. This creates a huge opportunity for entrepreneurs who can offer quality services at a competitive price. There's plenty of room for new notaries to enter the market and build a client base without taking anything away from other businesses. If you're interested in becoming a notary, now is the time to take action! <u>Take this as your "sign" to get started!</u>

There are many benefits to working as a notary, which we'll talk about in more detail in Chapter 2. You can choose your hours, working as little or as much as you want. This makes it a fantastic side hustle for those with full-time jobs or other commitments. Additionally, being a notary is a great way to strengthen your CV and prove yourself a valuable and contributing member of society. Unlike many other side hustles or part-time jobs, there is almost no limit to how much money you can earn as a notary. The more documents you notarize, the more you earn. You could easily make six figures in this industry with a little hard work and determination. Furthermore, being a notary does not require any special knowledge or training beyond what is required to become certified by your state. Anyone can become a notary with the right paperwork and commitment.

You'll learn how to expand your notary business and market your services effectively. We'll cover a range of strategies and options so that you can find the approach that best suits your needs. Whether you're looking to grow your client base or improve your marketing efforts, you'll have access to all the knowledge and tools you'll need to succeed. You'll also find a directory of state-by-state notary requirements (Chapter 5), so you can be sure you're following the relevant rules and regulations for your area.

Should you become interested in expanding your notary business into loan signings, this book provides a detailed guide to go above and beyond being a notary public. It also covers how to work from home in the ever-expanding remote online notary (RON) market.

During the COVID-19 pandemic, many states implemented emergency policies that allowed notaries to notarize documents electronically. This sparked a dramatic increase in the use of remote notary services. According to the National Notary Association, the number of notarizations conducted via video conferencing increased by an astounding 547% in 2020, compared with 2019. This is a huge benefit for notaries because it allows them to serve many clients without meeting in person.

How profitable is it? Let's consider a relatively conservative example. Imagine you can comfortably complete four loan signings per week. Each signing takes an average of four hours, but at $50 per hour, you're earning $200 per signing. You're now bringing in an additional $800 per week. Plus, because you can schedule your notary work in your own time, you are free to continue working at your current job.

If you're interested in becoming a notary, there's no time like the present. Becoming qualified as a notary is relatively easy and inexpensive and can be completed in just a few weeks. With some knowledge and effort, you can become a successful notary public and comfortably increase your income by $800 per week or more in the next few months.

I promise that with the advice and knowledge gained from this book, you will be fully equipped to run your own successful notary business in the shortest amount of time. This book contains all the information you'll need to get started, and will support you as you take your business from one level to the next. The information and advice provided inside is comprehensive and easy to understand, while being specific to each state.

With this book, you'll have everything you need. You won't need to go anywhere else for resources or support. Plus, I'll be here to support you every step of the way! You can find my email address at the back of the book.

The knowledge, skills, advice, and reference points in this book will turn you into an expert compared to the average person. Every chapter will provide you with valuable information that you can act on straight away. By following my advice, you will have everything you need to start earning money as a notary without having to pick up another book.

Follow the advice in this book, and you will be on your way to notarial success.

1

WHAT IS A NOTARY?

Notaries have a long and storied history dating back as far as ancient Egypt. Scribes would write down official communications to carry out their duties as prescribed by law or custom. It is from around this era that the first notary came into existence – a Roman slave named Tiro. He developed his system called "notae" which he used while taking notes on speeches made by Cicero, a famous orator. Tiro was later freed in 53 BC.

Fast forward to Columbus's time, when notaries often accompanied explorers on their voyages. The reigning monarch's King Ferdinand and Queen Isabella tasked notaries to be impartial witnesses to any agreements made between explorers and to ensure that all treasures found during a voyage were properly accounted for.

Appointed in 1639, Thomas Fugill was the American Colonies' first notary. However, he was soon removed from office after it was discovered that he had been falsifying documents. This led to a loss of trust in the notary system, and it was not until the late 1600s that the colonies began to appoint new notaries. Today, the notary system is an important part of American society, and its integrity is essential to maintaining the public's trust.

Shakespeare's time working with a Warwickshire Notary may have given him first-hand experience with the kind of legal disputes that are at the heart of the play, *The Merchant of Venice*. As an assistant to a notary, Shakespeare would have witnessed first-hand the drawing up of legal documents and the witnessing of signatures. This would have put him in direct contact with the kind of people who appear in the play, like moneylenders and merchants.

John Coolidge was 78 years old when he became a Notary Public. His son Calvin Coolidge was Vice President of the United States under President Warren G. Harding. When Harding died in 1923, Coolidge needed to be sworn in as the new President. The usual practice is for the President to be 'sworn in' by the Chief Justice of the Supreme Court. However, at the time, Chief Justice William Howard Taft was on vacation. Rather than wait for Taft to return, Coolidge's father administered the oath to his son. Calvin Coolidge holds the achievement of being the only U.S. President to have been sworn into office by a notary public.

Anyone interested in working as a notary public should ideally have a clear understanding of the different terms and titles that are used in the industry. Let's take a look at some of these distinctions now..

A **notary public** is an individual appointed by the government to serve as an official witness to the signing of important documents. Notaries are responsible for verifying the identity of the individual signing the document, and they must also ensure that the person understands the content of the document before putting their signature on it.

A **mobile notary** is a notary public offering to travel to meet with clients.

A **remote online notary** (RON) is a notary public who can perform notarizations electronically using audio-visual technology.

A **loan signing agent** (LSA), otherwise known as a notary signing agent (NSA), is a notary public who has been further trained to notarize mortgage paperwork, home refinancing, and related real estate transactions. This involves working with the borrower, real estate agents, escrow officers, and title companies to ensure that all documents are signed correctly and on time.

Loan signing agents must be able to understand and explain the documents to borrowers and ensure all documents are properly executed and notarized per state and federal law. They must undergo a background check and be bonded to qualify for this type of work. As a result, loan signing agents typically earn more money than notaries public.

While notary publics are tasked with witnessing the signing of important documents and verifying identity's of the signatories - they are not, however, allowed to give legal advice. They cannot answer questions about the document or the legal consequences of signing it. The same is true for loan signing agents who – while they may be asked to explain the document to the borrower – must decline to answer any questions about the legal implications of taking out the loan or carrying out any other transaction.

If you are intrigued about becoming a loan signing agent (LSA), turn to chapter 7 for more information on the requirements and qualifications needed for this position.

Notaries are responsible for a wide variety of tasks, but the two most common are witnessing signatures and administering oaths. To witness a signature, the notary must be present when the signer affixes their signature to the document in question. The notary then witnesses and confirms the identity of the signer, and notes their willingness to sign the document. The notary may also be required to verify that the document is legitimate and has been properly executed.

Notaries are typically used in situations where financial or legal documents are being executed. For example, a notary may witness the signing of a financial document such as a mortgage, loan, deed, or auto title transfer, or a legal document such as those relating to a custody agreement, will, trust, power of attorney, affidavit, or a contract for the sale of a home. In addition, notaries are often used in business transactions, such as the signing of a lease agreement or an employment contract, or the closing of a business deal.

Notaries can also administer oaths, which is the act of confirming that someone has sworn to tell the truth. Oaths are often used in legal proceedings, such as depositions or court hearings.

Each type of notary provides different services, and each is typically paid by a different party. Traditional notaries typically charge by the document or service, and are paid by the person whose signature they're notarizing. Mobile notaries travel to their clients, which may incur an additional fee, but as with traditional notaries, they are typically paid by the client per document.

As specially trained notaries who work with loan documents, loan signing agents are typically paid by the company who hired them, such as a signing service, title company, or lending institution. In general, however, it is the party who is requesting the notary services who pays the notary fee.

Notarization is the process that involves authenticating a document with the official seal of a notary public. Notarization gives each party peace of mind and ensures that everyone involved understands the terms of the contract. Notarization adds an extra layer of security to any transaction. In many cases, notarization is necessary in order to make a document legally binding. The notarization act attests to the fact that the document is genuine and that all signatures are valid. You'll also commonly hear of the need for documents to be "notarized" when applying for residence permits or for foreign passports abroad.

When a notary is presented with a document to sign, the first thing they must do is to require a personal appearance. This means that the individual signing the document must be physically in the presence of the notary. The notary must then verify the identity of the signer by asking for identification, such as a driver's license or passport.

Next, the notary public will verify that the document does not contain any blank spaces before checking the name on the document against the identification provided by the signer. If everything matches, the notary will check the certificate wording to ensure that the notarized document will be accepted by the intended recipient.

The third step is to ensure the individual signing the document is doing so of their own free will, and that they know what they are doing. The notary can then proceed with the notarization. The signer will be asked to swear or affirm that they have read and understand the document, and they will then be asked to sign it in front of the notary.

The fourth step of the process is recording a journal entry, which ensures that there is a record of the notarization in case it is later called into question. A journal entry is legally required in most states and is good practice, even if it is not required in your state.

Completing and signing the notarial certificate is the fifth and final step in the notarization process. This certificate serves as evidence that all the required steps were completed during the notarization process and provides important information about the transaction. It is an essential component of any notarized document.

A loan signing has additional steps beyond a standard notarization. For more information on loan signings, see chapter 7.

Notarization can be done remotely using video conferencing, but there are additional steps that must be followed. More information on Remote Online Notarizations can be found in chapter 8.

While notaries are most often employed in the banking and real estate industries, their skills are in demand across a wide range of industries. They may be employed by law firms to witness the signing of documents or by companies to notarize signatures on contracts. Many notaries specialize in providing services to private individuals.

Finally, let's explore some facts and statistics about America's booming notary business.

As of 2019, there were nearly 4.4 million notaries in the United States, notarizing more than 1.25 billion documents per year. For centuries, the role of the Notary Public was dominated by men, with women not permitted to become notaries in the United States until the early 1900s. Today, however, the landscape has changed dramatically. According to the National Notary Association, more than two-thirds of America's Notaries are now women.

Although it may seem as if "notary public" can be translated to "notario publico" in Spanish, these two roles are not the same. While a notary public may encounter legal documents when witnessing signatures or certifying copies, they are prohibited from providing legal advice. In many Latin American countries, however, a notario publico is a high-ranking person who has been specially trained and licensed to provide a range of legal services, including the preparation of legal documents and the representation of clients in court. So take your time with this difference.

The coronavirus pandemic had an unexpected effect on the notary industry. While businesses in other sectors struggled, notary businesses thrived. The pandemic lockdowns necessitated the rapid digitization of industries, and companies turned to notaries to help them safely and securely conduct their business online. The notary industry is well positioned to continue its rapid growth in the coming years as the world has adapted and overcome a global pandemic.

There is a clear hierarchy in the notary industry which you must also know. It is as follows. **All loan signing agents are notaries, but not all notaries are loan signing agents.** To become a loan signing agent, you must first become a notary public in your state. Certification as a loan signing agent is obtained by sitting an exam administered or approved by the Signing Professionals Workgroup (SPW).

The movie Pain & Gain provides a poignant example of the possible consequences of a fraudulent notarization. Based loosely on real events, the movie tells the story of gang members who attempt to extort a wealthy businessman, ultimately leading to their arrests. When Victor Kershaw is kidnapped by Daniel Lugo, John Mese (a notary public and Lugo's employer) is bribed to notarize documents in Kershaw's absence. The documents give Lugo power of attorney over Kershaw's assets. Lugo and his team, for a short time, enjoy Kershaw's mansion and extravagant lifestyle. Mese is later arrested and sentenced to 15 years in prison. The movie illustrates the importance of a notary being honest and above reproach.

2

WHY BECOME A NOTARY PUBLIC OR LOAN SIGNING AGENT?

There are many reasons to become a notary public or loan signing agent. Both professions offer opportunities for career growth and the possibility to work from home. As a notary public, you can provide important services to your community, such as document authentication and witnessing signatures. Loan signing agents have recently been in high demand due to the red-hot housing market, and can earn a good income by helping borrowers sign their loan documents. If you desire a rewarding career with flexible hours, becoming a notary public or loan signing agent may be the right choice for you!

There are a variety of factors which impact a notary's earnings, including their location, the type of work they do, and the number of hours they work. Therefore, it can be hard to generalize earnings in this field.

Employment specialists Indeed reported in 2018 that the average income for a notary public is $32,593. However, those working in a fixed setting like a bank, law firm, or government agency can earn significantly more, with Glassdoor reporting an average salary of $54,772 per year. It is also worth noting that many notaries are self-employed and therefore work on a freelance basis, which can further affect these figures.

The average hourly rate for a Notary Public is $15.87, according to the U.S. Bureau of Labor Statistics (BLS). However, those who work as freelance notaries can earn much more than this – sometimes up to $200 per hour. In general, the more experience and qualifications a notary has, the higher their earnings will be. Location also plays a role – Notaries in New York City, for example, tend to earn more than those in other parts of the country.

The type of work that a notary does can also affect their earnings. Those who provide mobile services or who specialize in complex documents may charge higher rates than those who only provide basic notary services. Ultimately, there is no one-size-fits-all answer to how much a notary can earn per year – it all depends on individual circumstances. In general, however, it is safe to say that a notary can earn a decent living.

Part-time work can be an awesome way to earn some extra cash. But what if you want to earn a full-time income? If you're considering a full-time career as a mobile Notary, you'll be pleased to know that according to *NNA's 2020 Notary Survey*, one in two mobile Notaries working full-time earn at least $2,000 per month. In fact, nearly two in every three respondents reported earning $4,000 or more per month, with **16 % earning $7,500 or more**. These figures demonstrate that a career as a full-time Notary can be a financially viable option, particularly for those interested in mobile work. With earning potential like that, it's no wonder that an increasing number of people are choosing to become mobile Notaries.

Many people become notaries because they want the flexibility to work part-time. In fact, according to the *National Notary Association's 2020 Notary Survey*, only 39 % of notaries work full-time. This leaves a significant portion of notaries who are working part-time. Part-time notaries are doing well, with many earning a steady income. The survey found that 43% of part-time notaries earn at least $500 per month, and almost 30% earn at least $1,000 per month. This is likely because part-time notaries have the flexibility to decide when and where they work, which allows them to pick up extra shifts or take on higher-paying jobs.

Loan signing agents (LSAs) are trained professionals who play a critical role in the mortgage industry by notarizing loan documents for borrowers. They typically earn a fee for each loan signing appointment, which can vary depending on the type of service.

While the job may seem straightforward, loan signing agents must be highly trained and knowledgeable to ensure that all documents are signed correctly. As a result, their services can be quite valuable. But how much do these professionals earn for their services? The answer, unfortunately, is more complex. Rates can vary significantly depending on their experience and the type of work they are performing.

LSAs who work for escrow offices typically earn more per appointment than those who work for loan signing services. Loan signing services typically pay $75-$125 per appointment, while escrow offices tend to pay more like $125-$200 per appointment. In addition to their fees, LSAs may also receive reimbursements for travel expenses and notary supplies. As such, LSAs can expect to earn a sizable income from their appointments. Assuming you take on 50 loan signing appointments per month, you could earn between $4,000 and $6,000 per month.

As another example, if you had limited time and only took on 320 loan signing appointments in a year, you could still earn a significant amount – as much as $1,000 to $1,500 per month. Of course, earnings will depend on a number of factors, including the location of the loan signing appointments, the type of loan being signed, and the length of time it takes to complete each appointment. However, taking on a large volume of loan signings can certainly be a lucrative way to earn a living.

In short, LSAs are an essential part of the mortgage process, and their earnings reflect the importance of their work.

Let's assume that loan signing agents can earn an average of $100 per loan signing appointment. Appointments usually take 1-2 hours to complete, and may require additional travel time. If a loan signing agent works part-time and comfortably completes 5 appointments per week, they can expect to earn $500 per week, or $2,000 per month for up to ten hours of work. If the appointments are scheduled through an escrow office, the loan signing agent may also receive an additional $50 per appointment. In this case, they would earn as much as $750 per week, or $3,000 per month for the same 10 hours of work.

It is common for a full-time LSA to complete 15 assignments per week. This can take approximately 30-45 hours to complete, which includes travel time. If the LSA charges an average of $100 per appointment, they can earn $1,500 per week or $6,000 per month. **If the work comes from an escrow office**, they may also get an extra $50 per appointment. That would bring their weekly earnings up to $2,250 and their monthly earnings up to $9,000. This is a 50% raise with no extra time or effort required. This is why it's so important to learn how to get escrow business directly. You must learn to approach escrow officers, real estate agents, and mortgage loan officers.

As with most professions, experience is a big factor in how much you can earn as a notary. Notaries who have been in the business for years are able to command higher fees than those who are just starting out. This is because experienced notaries have developed a reputation for being reliable and knowledgeable. They also have a greater understanding of the notary process and are able to complete documents more quickly. As a result, they are able to take on more clients and earn more money.

While new notaries may earn less than their experienced counterparts, they can still command respectable fees if they are able to complete assignments quickly and efficiently, as well as by marketing their services effectively. With time and experience, new notaries can expect to see their earnings increase.

To maximize your earnings as a notary, it is important to treat being a notary as a career. This means being in it for the long haul, keeping up to date with the industry, and continually improving your skills. Ultimately, whether or not you are able to make a success out of being a notary will depend on how much time and dedication you are willing to put into it. With experience and dedication, you can become a top-earning notary who commands high fees for your services.

The best notaries earn more than average notaries because they offer a higher level of service. They are able to work quickly and efficiently, and they have a deep understanding of the notary process. In addition, the best notaries can build strong relationships with their clients. They take their time to get to know their clients and understand their needs. As a result, their clients trust them and are willing to pay a premium for their services.

The best notaries are those who offer a wide range of services. In addition to notarizing documents, there are a variety of other services that notaries can offer to increase their income. By diversifying their offerings, they are able to attract more clients and earn more money. According to the NNA, in 2020, around 76% of notaries also offered loan signings, and 30% took on non-notary work, such as the following..

· I-9 services, which involve verifying the identity and employment eligibility of individuals who are applying for jobs in the United States.

· Courier services, which involve transporting documents and packages from one location to another.

· Field inspections, which can involve observing a property or location or witnessing the signing of documents or the delivery of goods.

· Apostille services, which involve authenticating documents for use in foreign countries. This complex service is further discussed in Chapter 8.

· Fingerprinting, which is a process of taking an individual's fingerprints on behalf of the authorities.

· Notaries who are trained and credentialed to provide these services can charge higher fees for their services.

· Mobile notaries are notaries who travel to their clients rather than having the clients come to them - this can be convenient for clients who have busy schedules or who live far from a stationary notary. Mobile notaries tend to make more money than stationary notaries because they can charge for their travel time and expenses. As long as these fees are reasonable, most clients will be happy to pay a notary's travel expenses to avoid the hassle of having to travel to a stationary notary.

Any business, including a notary business, can increase its volume and income by networking. Keeping up with industry trends, attending industry conferences and workshops through the National Notary Association (NNA) and the American Society of Notaries, and making the public aware of notary services are all ways to increase business volume and income.

Marketing your notary services to the public is essential for bringing in new clients. There are many ways to do this, such as distributing flyers, placing advertisements in local publications, or getting involved in the community. By being involved, a notary shows that they are invested in their community and are more likely to be trusted with important tasks like notarizing documents. This will be discussed more in Chapter 6.

The United States Bureau of Labor Statistics estimates that the mean annual salary for a notary public is $39,490. However, this figure needs to take into account the dramatic variation in earnings that can be seen from state to state. Some states boast salaries well above the national average, while others offer salaries that are closer to the average. For example, Notaries in New York State earn a mean annual salary of almost $53,000, while those in Orlando, Florida earn just over $26,000 on average. The reason for this discrepancy is largely due to the differing cost of living in different states. States with the highest cost of living, such as California or New York, tend to offer higher salaries to public notaries in order to compensate for the increased cost of living. Conversely, in states with a low cost of living, such as Florida, notaries can live by the beach on a lower salary.

The same is true for notaries who work in urban areas versus rural areas. Due to the higher cost of living in cities, urban notaries tend to earn more than their rural counterparts.

According to the United States Census Bureau, the median per capita income in 2020 was $35,384. As a notary, it is possible to easily surpass this figure, even working part-time. In fact, the full earning potential as a notary can easily reach six figures.

Some famous notaries include:

· Samuel Clemens (aka Mark Twain) was an American writer and humorist best known for his novel The Adventures of Tom Sawyer - Clemens was also a qualified notary.

· Jennifer Lopez is an American actress, singer, and dancer who has starred in popular films such as Selena and Out of Sight. Prior to achieving her celebrity status, Lopez worked as a notary.

· Stanley Tucci is an American actor, writer, producer, and director who has appeared in popular films like The Devil Wears Prada/The Hunger Games, and has also held a notary certificate.

· Joe Moeller is an American baseball player who famously pitched for the LA Dodgers, and has also held notary qualifications.

· Christa McAuliffe was an American astronaut who was selected to participate in the Space Shuttle Challenger mission, and a notary.

· The first notary to be commissioned in all fifty states was Klaus Hergescheimer.

As a notary, one of the great advantages you enjoy is the ability to set your own schedule. This can be a great benefit if you have other commitments, such as children that make it difficult to adhere to a traditional work schedule. Ultimately, choosing your own schedule as a notary gives you the freedom to work on your own terms.

One of the most common questions people have about notaries is how much they charge for their services. While notaries are public officials, they are also business owners, and as such, they are able to keep all of the revenue they generate from providing their services. While fees vary depending on the type of service being provided and the location, most notaries charge by the document, with the average fee falling between $5 and $15. A notary transaction usually takes just a few minutes to complete. It is often the case that a client will need more than one document witnessed at a time.

In most states, there are limits imposed on how much a notary can charge for their services, with California and Nevada imposing the highest maximum fee of $15 per document. At the lower end, notaries in Georgia and New York can charge only $2 per document and only $1 in Illinois. Some states, such as Alaska, Louisiana, and Vermont, do not impose any limits.

While these limits help to ensure that notaries are providing their services at a fair price, they can also make it harder for them to earn a proper wage. For this reason, many notaries also offer loan signing services, which tend to be more lucrative - as mentioned earlier.
Being a notary is much more than signing and stamping paperwork. As a notary, you play an impor-

tant role in society. You are also an important part of stopping identity theft and other related crimes. Notaries help to ensure that documents are authentic and that the people signing them are who they say they are. This protects businesses and individuals from fraudsters who would otherwise take advantage of them. As a notary, your earning potential is effectively limitless. This makes being a notary a great option for those who want to set their own hours. In addition, having "notary public" on your CV looks great to potential employers. It shows that you are responsible and trustworthy.

The tax benefits of being a notary are also very advantageous. As a notary, you are a 1099 independent contractor, which means you are self-employed. This has many taxation benefits. This means that you are able to take advantage of many beneficial self-employment tax laws, and can deduct many of your business expenses from your taxes. This is much better than being a W-2 employee.

When people consider becoming a notary, they often focus on the potential upsides: the flexible hours, the possibility of working from home, and the relatively low cost of starting a notary business. However, there are also a number of downsides that potential notaries should be aware of.

Firstly, the income can be very irregular, and it can be hard to make a living solely off of notarizing documents. Many clients only need notary services on an occasional basis. Additionally, making even a small mistake as a notary can be quite costly - you could be sued for thousands of dollars if something goes wrong. As a result, it is important to have an error and omission (E&O) insurance policy to protect yourself financially. Finally, there are initial startup costs associated with becoming a notary, including the cost of bonding and certification, depending on the area in which you live.

Although being a notary comes with some risks, these risks can be mitigated by taking the time to thoroughly understand the responsibilities of the role. If you are looking for an interesting and rewarding career, then being a notary is certainly worth considering.

3
WHAT IS REQUIRED – AND HOW MUCH DOES IT COST?

When starting any business, it is important to consider all of the costs you will incur, both at the start and ongoing. This is especially true for a notary business, as there are a number of required fees and supplies. It is possible to get your notary business up and running for as little as $800. However, it is also common for people to spend closer to $2,000 on their initial costs. If you are thinking about becoming a notary or loan signing agent, ensure you consider all of the potential expenditures before making your decision.

In chapter 7, you can find a list of supplies and equipment you'll need, as well as the prices of each.

For the credit savvy among you, consider applying for a business credit card before incurring any expenses relating to your new notary business. When you put your expenses on a business credit card, you can often get cash back or points that you can use for travel or discounts. Additionally, by putting your expenses on a business card, you will be keeping your personal and business expenses separate, which will make your accounting and bookkeeping much simpler. For people with bad credit history, this is a bad idea as you'll likely incur debt for late payments.

Overall, there are many good reasons to start a notary business, and the startup costs are relatively low compared to other businesses.

When becoming a notary, there are numerous steps that you are required to take – with each step having a corresponding cost. Depending on the state in that you live, you may need to take mandatory courses, pass exams, and get fingerprinted. The fees for each of these range from a few dollars to a few hundred dollars.

Some states do require you to take a mandatory education course which can cost approximately $50, followed by an exam for approximately $40. The passport photo will cost approximately $15. Live scan fingerprints will cost approximately $40. A background check may also be required by some states for an additional cost of $50.

These are just some of the initial costs associated with becoming a notary public. More detailed information regarding these procedures and their costs can be found in Chapters 4 and Chapter 5 of this book.

In order to qualify as a notary, you must first be commissioned by your state. The cost of becoming a notary varies from state to state, but it can range from approximately $100 to more than $500. Depending on the state, this cost may include a filing fee, a bond, a background check, and any required training and exams.

In order to work as a loan signing agent, you must first be commissioned as a notary. Loan signing agents are not required to be certified by law, but many title companies and lenders require certification before they will work with a loan signing agent. Certification proves that the loan signing agent has been trained in loan signings and is familiar with the required procedures. There are a variety of ways to become certified, including online courses and in-person training. The cost of certification varies, but it is generally less than $200. In addition to the initial cost of becoming a notary public or certified loan signing agent, there may also be annual fees for renewing your commission or certification. These fees are generally less than $100 per year.

There are a few popular and reputable loan signing agent training courses, such as NSA Certification by the National Notary Association, the Loan Signing System, and Notary2Pro. The cost of loan signing agent training generally ranges from approximately $70 to $500, depending on the course, the provider, and its associated materials.

Some states have additional requirements for loan signing agents, such as Minnesota, which requires loan signing agents to have a closing agent license. Similarly, Indiana and Maryland require title insurance licenses for all closings. In addition, some companies may have their own specific requirements for loan signing agents. Still, with the right training and preparation, loan signing agents can play an important role in ensuring the smooth completion of real estate transactions.

The process of becoming a notary varies between states. Some states have minimal requirements, while others require training and/or an exam. It is important to check the requirements in your state before beginning the process. The requirements can be found on the Secretary of State's website in your state. As long as you are aware of the requirements in your state, the process of becoming a notary should be straightforward.

In Arizona, for example, the process consists of three simple steps: completing an application form, getting it notarized, and posting it with $25 for a $5,000 bond and a $43 application fee. The whole process can be completed in a few weeks. In California, however, the process is slightly different. In addition to the above steps, California notaries are required to undertake training, pass an exam, and have their fingerprints taken.

Once you have met each of the requirements for your state, you can begin the application process. Once your application has been submitted, it typically takes a few weeks to receive your commission in the mail. Note that you may be required to renew your commission every year or two, so be sure to check your state's requirements periodically.

In some states, there are restrictions on who can perform loan closings. For example, in Connecticut, the rules about who can conduct closings for most mortgage loans require that the closing be conducted by a licensed attorney, unless the loan doesn't require a title insurance policy to be issued.

In Delaware, Georgia, and Massachusetts, meanwhile, an attorney who is admitted to the state bar must be present during the closing of property transactions. And in New York, the rules state that companies who employ signing professionals to perform loan closings may choose to only work with licensed attorneys. South Carolina has similar rules to Delaware, requiring an attorney to at least be present during a loan signing.

South Dakota's rules are worryingly ambiguous, with a large amount of confusion as to whether Loan Signing Agents who are not also attorneys can conduct loan signings. In Texas specifically, home equity line of credit (HELOC) loan signings must occur in the office of a title company, attorney, or lender.

Vermont and West Virginia are two more states where an attorney admitted to the state bar must be present during the closing of a real property transaction. These differences make it vitally important to check the rules about who can perform loan closings in your state before you proceed with your application to become a loan signing agent.

In the United States, there are certain states that are considered "attorney states." This means that an attorney must be present in order for legal services to be provided. This can have implications for loan closings, as an attorney may need to be present in order to ensure that all of the required documentation is in order.

The following states are attorney states:

• Alabama

• Hawaii

• Iowa

• Kentucky

• Maine

• Mississippi

• New Hampshire

• North Dakota

• Rhode Island

- Tennessee

- Virginia.

While the rules can change from time to time, generally speaking, if a notary lives in one of the above states, they will need to make sure that an attorney is present during the closing of a loan.

It is advisable to make your own inquiries with your state's Secretary of State's office and with local attorneys to find out the standard practice for loan signings. It is possible that you may still have some role to play.

A **notary bond**, also known as a surety bond - is a three-party agreement between the principal (the notary), the surety (the bonding company), and the obligee (the entity who requires the bond). The bonded notary is financially responsible for any damages resulting from losses due to fraudulent or criminal acts, errors, or omissions while performing notarial duties. Notary bonds are required by most states in order to become a notary public.

The cost of a notary bond depends on various factors, including the coverage amount required, the notary's geographical location, credit score, financial history, and type of practice. For example, a Notary with good credit and a clean financial history can expect to pay approximately $50 for a four-year term.

The process of obtaining a surety bond as a notary typically takes a few days at the most and requires the completion of an application, payment of the premium, and review by the bonding company. After the bond has been approved and issued, it is then mailed to the notary. In many instances, a notary can receive approval on the day of their application and receive the bond itself the following business day.

A notary bond covers the Notary public for losses arising out of fraudulent or dishonest acts, errors, or omissions while performing notarial duties. This coverage is different from traditional insurance policies in that it protects the public rather than the individual notary. Therefore, it is important to understand the purpose of a notary bond before assuming that it will provide full protection against all risks. On the other hand, E&O (errors and omissions) insurance is designed to protect the notary, as we'll discuss in a second.

Different states have their own requirements when it comes to notary bonds. In California, for example, all notaries are required to have a $15,000 bond in place over a four-year term. In Texas and Pennsylvania, the bond amount is slightly lower at $10,000 over four years. In Florida, standard notaries are required to have a $7,500 bond in place over four years, while remote online notaries must have a $25,000 bond. There are some states where there is no requirement for a notary bond at all, such as New York and Georgia.

And in Illinois, the bond requirement is $5,000 over four years. These are just some examples of the variation of notary bond requirements from state to state. Full details can be found in Chapter 5.

In many states, Notaries are required by law to purchase a Notary surety bond before they can begin performing notarizations. The goal of the bond is to protect the public from any financial harm that may result from negligent mistakes or intentional misconduct by the notary while doing their duties, as we just mentioned.

However, the surety bond is not designed to protect the notary. If a claim was made against your notary bond, you are forced, by law, to pay it back. You may also be held personally liable for any costs above the amount of your bond, including court fees, legal fees, and any other expenses.

As a result, it is important for Notaries to have both a bond and an errors and omissions (E&O) insurance policy in place. The benefit of having a Notary bond and an E&O Insurance policy is that your insurance policy could protect against losses on your Notary bond that you would otherwise be required to repay yourself.

As a notary, you are responsible for ensuring that all documents are completed correctly and in accordance with state law. Errors and omissions insurance (E&O) is a type of insurance that helps protect notaries against financial losses arising from errors/omissions while performing their professional duties. Sometimes referred to as professional indemnity insurance, an errors and omissions insurance policy protects you in the event that a mistake is made, and the customer suffers financial damages as a result. E&O insurance can cover losses such as damages awarded in a lawsuit, settlements reached out of court, and legal fees associated with defending a claim.

While notaries are not legally required to carry E&O insurance, many escrow companies require loan signing agents to have policy amounts of at least $25,000. Some companies may require much higher policy amounts, such as $100,000. The cost of E&O insurance varies from state to state, but a $25,000 policy might cost approximately $20 to $40 per year, while a $100,000 policy might cost approximately $100 to $175 per year - roughly the income of one loan signing.

Loan signing agents have a vital role in the mortgage loan signing process by ensuring that all documents are properly signed and notarized. They are also tasked with ensuring that the borrower understands the documents they are signing and that they are signing them freely and willingly.

Loan signing agents have access to private financial information, which is why the mortgage industry requires an annual background screening for all loan signing agents. This background screening includes a residence and identity verification, criminal history check, a driving record check, a check of the Office of Foreign Assets Control (OFAC) register, as well as a review of any past financial bankruptcies or foreclosures. The background screening goes back seven years in some states and ten years for county, state, and federal records.

The search of public records includes a search of your Social Security Number, court records, the criminal database, and driving and motor vehicle records. The Terrorist Watch List and National Sex Offender register are also assessed. Dismissals, expungements, and pardons will not appear in a background screening.

Points are assigned to each individual criminal or driving offense, with more serious offenses carrying more points. For example, a non-moving violation attracts 2 points, while robbery carries 25 points. To pass the background check and be permitted to work as a loan signing agent, applicants must reach a total score of fewer than 25 points. If you opt-out of the background screening, many title service companies, and mortgage companies will choose not to work with you as a loan signing agent.

When becoming a notary, there are several important supplies and pieces of equipment that you will need to purchase. Perhaps the most important item on the list is a laser dual-tray printer that can handle both legal and letter-sized paper. This is essential for printing out documents related to your work as a notary. You can expect to pay around $300-$500 for a high-quality printer. If you're happy to use a refurbished model, you may be able to find a good-quality machine for around half this price. Another important item is, of course, the paper. You will need to have reams of both legal and letter-sized paper on hand for printing out documents related to your work. A ream of paper usually costs around $5-$6. Buying in bulk brings down the price. A small portable scanner can be a helpful tool, allowing you to digitize documents for easy storage. A small portable scanner typically costs around $70-$120, while a larger scanner can cost upwards of $400.

In addition to equipment, there are also several other supplies that you will need to purchase as a notary. One of the most important is an unlimited cell phone plan. This is necessary in order to be available to clients at all times. Unlimited cell phone plans typically cost around $50-$100 per month. A reliable car is also necessary, as you will often be called upon to travel to different locations. You should budget for gas, oil changes, and other routine maintenance costs. The financial cost of owning and maintaining a car varies depending on the make and model of the vehicle. Finally, you will need a bag or briefcase to store all of your supplies. A simple leather briefcase should suffice and can be purchased for under $100.

A notary journal is a bound book in which a notary public records all of the official acts performed during their tenure in office. In many states, notaries are required by law to maintain a journal, and it provides an important record of their official acts. A notary journal typically records critical details about each notarization, such as the names/addresses of the parties involved, the date/time of the notarization, the type of document being notarized, any witnesses present, and whether any special instructions were given. In some states, the journal is also used to collect information about the person requesting the notarization, including their photo ID, signature, and thumbprint. A notary journal ensures the integrity of the notarial process and protects both the notary and the signer from potential fraud or disputes. Notary journals typically cost between $10-$15. Please make sure you purchase official journals, not knock-offs from Amazon.

Extra notary certificates can be used if a document to be notarized does not have sufficient room for a notary seal or lacks the required notary language. The notary can attach a copy of their notary certificate to the document in lieu of their normal seal or stamp. Notaries should always keep extra notary certificates with them in case the need for one arises. Bundles of 50 copies can usually be purchased for under $10.

An inkless thumb printer is a device that allows a notary to take an imprint of a person's thumb without using ink. These small devices are relatively inexpensive, usually starting from around $15.

Notaries can find relevant state-specific requirements and supplies at websites such as asnnotary.org/?form=supplies.

A notary stamp is a self-inking rubber stamp that holds the official seal and commission information of a notary public. It is used to authenticate documents that require the signature of a notary. The cost of a notary stamp varies depending on the state where you live, but expect to pay upwards of $15 for the stamp.

A metal embosser seal is a raised stamp that is also used to authenticate certain niche documents, such as a document relating to a foreign transaction. The embosser contains the notary's name, commission number, and expiration date. The cost of a metal embosser seal is around $30.

Notary stamps and seals differ depending on your state because each state sets its own requirements for notaries. The process for getting a notary seal varies from state to state. In most states, you must be a commissioned Notary Public before you can order your notary seal.

As a notary, you are in the business of providing essential services to the public. In order to be successful, notaries need to be proactive in marketing themselves and their businesses. There are various things to consider when it comes to marketing costs. First, you will need business cards. These can be purchased from any office supply store or ordered from an inline printer. You can expect to pay between $10 and $30 for 100 business cards. You will also need a website. You should expect to pay around $100 per year for web hosting and domain registration.

Additionally, you should consider listing yourself in directories such as Notary Café, Notary Stars, Notary Rotary, the National Notary Association's directory Signing Agent, and 123Notary. Some of these directories offer a free listing that can be upgraded later for better visibility and exposure, while others don't offer a free plan.

Finally, notaries should budget for ongoing education and innovation, as this is essential for staying ahead of the competition. By investing in marketing and education, notaries can increase their visibility, attract new clients, and grow their businesses.

As a notary, you have the chance to choose from several different corporate structures for your business. The type of structure you choose will depend on the size and scope of your business, your personal liability risk, and your tax situation. Each structure has its own pros and cons, so it's important to carefully consider your options before deciding.

For example, a sole proprietorship is the simplest (and most common) business structure, but it offers no personal liability protection. On the other hand, a corporation offers legal protections and tax benefits, but it's more complex to set up and maintain. If you're just getting started, it may make sense to choose a simple structure like a sole proprietorship. But as your business grows, you may want to consider incorporating it to protect yourself from liability.

You should consult with a qualified tax advisor or attorney before making a decision. Ultimately, the best corporate structure for your notary business is the one that best meets your needs and objectives.

Notaries are often self-employed and operate as sole proprietors. A sole proprietorship is defined as a business owned and operated by a single individual. There are several advantages of operating as a **sole proprietor** as a notary. Firstly, it is relatively easy to set up and maintain a sole proprietorship. There is no need to file any special paperwork with the government or to obtain any licenses or permits. Secondly, a sole proprietor has complete control over the business. The sole proprietor can make all decisions about the business, including decisions about pricing, hiring, and marketing. Third, operating as a sole proprietor can be less expensive than other business structures.

There are also some disadvantages of operating as a sole proprietor for a notary. First, the sole proprietor is held liable for all debts and obligations of the business. This means that if the business was to fail, the sole proprietor might be held responsible for the repayment of debts. Second, investors may be reluctant to invest in a business with only one owner because they have less control over the direction of the company. Finally, sole proprietorships can be more difficult to sell than other types of businesses.

A **partnership** is a legal business arrangement where two or more people share ownership of the company. In a business context, partnerships are often formed in order to pool resources and expertise and to share the risks/rewards of business ventures. Partnerships can be either formal or informal, and they offer a number of advantages for businesses, including shared risk and increased capital. For a notary, partnering with another notary could be a way to expand the scope of their business. By teaming up with another notary, they would reach a larger client base and maybe offer more services. In addition, partners can provide valuable support and advice, which can be helpful in managing the challenges of running a notary business.

However, there are also some disadvantages, such as the potential for disagreements between partners and the need to follow formal procedures when making decisions. In addition, each partner is legally responsible for the debts and liabilities of the partnership, which could put personal assets at risk if the business encounters financial difficulties. For these reasons, you should determine whether a partnership is the right business structure for a notary business before entering into any agreements.

A limited liability company, or LLC, is a common structure that offers its owners some protection from personal liability of the LLC's debts. LLCs can be formed by one or more individuals, and they are often used by small businesses. Notaries are considered to be small business owners, and as such, they may find that an LLC is a good business structure for them.

One of the main benefits for a notary is that it can help to shield the notary's personal assets from liability for any professional negligence claims that may arise. This means that if the LLC was sued, the owner's personal assets would not be at risk. Another advantage of LLCs is that they can provide some flexibility in how the business is taxed. An LLC gives you the option of being taxed as an S corporation, which can simplify your taxes.

On the other hand, there are some drawbacks here. One of the main ones is that it is more expensive to set up and maintain. In addition, LLCs are subject to certain regulations and record-keeping requirements, which may be burdensome for a small business owner. The organizational structure of your notary business will have big implications for everything from your taxes to your personal liability. That's why it's important to choose the best business structure from the beginning. So, which is the right choice for your notary business?

There's no one-size-fits-all answer. The right decision will depend on the intended size and scope of your business, your financial situation, and your personal preferences. However, an LLC is often a good choice for businesses that are looking for more protection from liability.

An **S corporation** is a unique type of business structure that offers certain tax advantages. Like other types of business entities, an S corporation limits the liability of its owners. However, S corporations also have the added benefit of pass-through taxation, meaning that the profits or losses of the business are passed through to the shareholders, who then report these on their individual tax returns.

In order to qualify, the S corporation must have no more than 100 shareholders - and they must be U.S. citizens or residents. Because S corporations have stricter rules and regulations, they can be more expensive and complex to set up and maintain. Finally, S Corporations are subject to additional regulations, which can add to the overall complexity of the business.

A **corporation** is a legal entity which is separated from, and distinct from its owners. One advantage of a corporation is that it offers limited liability protection for its shareholders. In the case of a notary business, this means that the personal assets of the shareholders would be protected in the event that the business is sued. Another advantage of a corporation is that it can raise capital by selling shares of its stock.

While this is a significant advantage, there are also some disadvantages to consider. One downside of a corporation is that it is subject to double taxation, meaning that the corporation first pays taxes on its profits, and then the shareholders must pay taxes again when they receive dividends. Corporations are subject to more stringent regulations than LLCs, and this can make it more difficult and expensive to comply with the law. In addition, corporations can be complex and expensive to set up and maintain.

There are some important differences between corporations and LLCs. LLCs are not necessitated to have a board of directors or hold annual shareholder meetings, nor are they subject to the same level of scrutiny from state and federal regulators. For a notary business, an LLC may be a better option because it offers many of the same benefits as a corporation, with less paperwork and fewer fees.

Tax deductions are a fantastic way to save money on your taxes. As a notary, there are a few potential deductions that you may be able to take advantage of. For example, you can claim the cost of supplies, as well as any training or education expenses. You may also be able to deduct rent if you lease an office, or travel expenses if you incur them while conducting notarial business. You should always consult with a tax professional to determine which deductions you may be eligible for, as well as a legal professional when it comes to choosing your business structure.

4

BECOMING CERTIFIED AS A NOTARY PUBLIC OR LOAN SIGNING AGENT (STATE-BY-STATE)

Notary Public

In order to become a notary, many states ask you to take and pass an examination, while other states simply require that you fill out an application and pay a fee. While many states do not require any training or exams, **some states have specific requirements to be met to become a notary**. It is vital to check your state's requirements for becoming a notary public since they can vary and change over time.

· In **Alabama**, it is at the discretion of the appointing county probate judge whether or not someone is required to take a course and/or pass an exam before becoming a notary.

· In **Arkansas**, applicants have to achieve at least 80% in a multiple-choice exam to become a notary.

· In **California**, you have to take a six-hour training course and then score at least 70% in an exam.

· **Colorado** requires that applicants take and pass a course and exam, while **Connecticut** only requires that applicants pass an exam.

· In **Florida**, you have to complete a three-hour course.

· To become a notary in **Hawaii**, you must pass an in-person exam with a score of at least 80%. The exam is closed-book, and you must take it within one year of filing your application. You also have to take at least three courses during your 8-year notary commission.

· In **Illinois**, the rules are in the middle of changing, and soon, notaries will need to take an online course and take an exam.

· In **Indiana**, you have to score at least 80% on an exam in order to be a notary, and you also have to take at least three courses during your 8-year notary commission.

· In **Louisiana**, you have to pass an exam to become a notary, but attorneys are exempt from this requirement.

· In **Maine**, you must pass a written exam.

· In **Maryland**, you have to take a course, and then pass an exam.

· In **Massachusetts**, you are required to read General Laws Chapter 222 and agree to comply with its terms to become a notary.

· In **Michigan**, potential notaries are required to read the Michigan Notary Public Act before working as a notary.

· In **Missouri**, you are required to achieve at least 80% in an exam, while in **Montana**, you are required to complete four hours of training and achieve at least 80% in an exam.

· **Nebraska** requires that you achieve at least 85% in an exam, and **Nevada** requires that you take a three-hour course and then pass an exam.

· In **New Jersey**, you must take a course and pass an exam, though these requirements only came into place in October 2022.

· **New Mexico** requires that you take a course and achieve at least 80% in an exam to become a notary.

· In order to become a notary in **New York**, you must pass an in-person exam. The exam is closed-book, meaning that you will not be able to use any reference materials during the test. However, there are a few exemptions to this rule — attorneys and some court clerks are not required to take the exam.

· In **North Carolina**, the process is slightly different. In addition to taking a six-hour course at a local community college, you must also achieve a score of at least 80% on an examination. If you are an attorney, you are exempt from this requirement.

· In **Ohio**, you must take a three-hour course and pass an exam. Like in North Carolina, attorneys are exempt from this requirement.

· **Oregon** has an online examination process that you must complete before becoming a notary.

· Similarly, in **Pennsylvania**, you must complete a course and take an examination.

· In **Utah** and **Vermont**, you must simply pass an exam.

· In **Washington, DC**, you have to complete an in-person orientation session after submitting your application.

· In **West Virginia**, you are required to read The West Virginia Code, Chapter 39, Article 4.

· In **Wisconsin**, you must complete a tutorial and score at least 90% on an exam to become a notary.

· In **Wyoming**, you have to take a course and achieve at least 70% on an exam.

While all other states do not require any training or exams, it is important to check your state's requirements anyway because things can change.

A notary is a public officer, specifically appointed by the government, who is authorized to witness signatures and certify documents. A loan signing agent is a further qualified notary public who specializes in witnessing loan documents. Loan signing agents must be knowledgeable about loan terminology, understand the loan process, and be able to answer questions that borrowers may have about the loan process.

While both notaries and loan signing agents are responsible for witnessing signatures and certifying documents, loan signing agents have additional training and experience in handling loan documents. As a result, they are better equipped to assist borrowers with questions and ensure that all required documents are properly completed.

While there are some similarities between the professions, there are also some important differences. One key difference is in the way that each can charge for their services. Notaries are constrained by a list of maximum fees, while loan signing agents are able to negotiate their own fees. This means that loan signing agents have more flexibility when it comes to setting their prices. While there is no set maximum fee for loan signings, most agents charge between $100 and $200 per loan signing.

Certified Loan Signing Agents

In order to work as a loan signing agent, you must first be a commissioned notary. This is because loan signing agents are responsible for ensuring that all documents related to a loan are properly notarized. Without a valid commission, a notary would not be able to authenticate the signatures on these documents. If you're thinking about qualifying as a loan signing agent, it's important to understand the laws in your state. In some states, notaries can't work as loan signing agents, and in others, an attorney must be present during a loan signing.

For more information on state-specific requirements, please refer to the following chapter of this book.

Before becoming a loan signing agent, it is advisable to check your state's requirements in order to ensure compliance with all applicable laws. Taking a course to become a certified loan signing agent is not mandatory, but there are several benefits to doing so. First, it demonstrates that you have a knowledge of the loan signing process and are capable of completing documents accurately. Second, certification helps you stand out from the competition and make you more attractive to potential employees. In addition, many companies prefer and will only hire certified loan signing agents, as it shows that you are committed to your profession and are willing to invest in your own development. While becoming certified as a loan signing agent is not required, it is certainly beneficial and gives you a competitive edge over others.

Companies in the mortgage finance industry are subject to strict laws and regulations. In order to do business, these companies must comply with federal, state, and local laws and regulations. Companies that contract Signing Agents for home loan closings are required by the Consumer Financial Protection Bureau to have these professionals certified and background screened in order to meet compliance requirements for third-party service providers hired by financial institutions. By ensuring that their employees or contractors are properly trained, these companies better protect both themselves and their customers from any potential legal or financial liabilities.

Once you have passed your exam, you will be able to apply for certification from the National Notary Association. This certification will show potential employers that you are qualified to work as a loan signing agent. As a loan signing agent, you will learn how to prepare loan documents for signing, how to conduct loan signings, and how to notarize loan documents. You will also learn about the loan closing process, including how to explain the process to borrowers and answer their questions. You will also learn about the many different types of loans, such as adjustable-rate mortgages, balloon mortgages, and federal housing administration loans. In addition, you will learn about the different types of loan documents, such as promissory notes and security instruments.

By taking a loan signing agent course, you will gain the knowledge and skills you need to provide a valuable service to borrowers. Additionally, you will learn about proper notarization procedures and how to spot common errors in loan documents. By the end of your course, you will have the knowledge and skills necessary to work confidently as a loan signing agent. Companies that are looking to hire loan signing agents often place a great deal of importance on certification.

The process of becoming a certified loan signing agent generally takes one to two weeks. However, much of this time is typically spent waiting for the results of your background screening. Once you have completed the certification process and have passed your background check, you will be able to begin working as a loan signing agent. The cost of becoming an LSA varies depending on several factors, including the state you live in, whether you are already commissioned as a notary, and whether you already have appropriate insurance. The cost also depends on your choice of training and exam provider, as well as any licensing fees that may be required in certain states. Later in the book, you'll see examples of how much different packages cost.

The length of time it takes to finish a loan signing agent course, and certification exam can vary depending on the provider. For example, the NNA's

Notary Signing Agent course takes only a few hours & their exam consists of 45 multiple-choice questions, whereas a course from the Loan Signing System contains over twenty hours of total training.

Loan signing agents play a critical role in notarizing mortgage documents. They are responsible for ensuring that all documents are signed and witnessed properly and that all loan terms are met. If proper procedures are followed, they can avoid significant legal risks. They could be sued by the borrower for negligence or breach of contract, or they could be held liable for any losses incurred by the lender as a result of improper loan document handling. As such, it is essential for certified loan signing agents to understand their responsibilities and the risks they face. In addition, they should be familiar with the loan process and the documents involved. By taking these precautions, loan signing agents can help to ensure that loans are completed smoothly and without incident.

Loan document signings are important transactions that usually involve hundreds of thousands of dollars. As such, it is essential that loan Signing Agents follow their state's commission laws as well as federal mortgage regulations. In order to avoid such mistakes, Signing Agents should take the time to understand the laws and regulations governing loan document signings. They should also consider taking a course on Notary law.

Although it is not always required by law, many experts strongly recommend that loan signing agents purchase an errors and omissions (E&O) insurance policy. This type of insurance covers damages resulting from unintentional mistakes and can provide vital financial protection in the event of a claim. The Signing Professionals Workgroup (SPW) is an industry standards organization that recommends Signing Agents carry a minimum E&O policy of $25,000. This recommendation is based on a study that found most claims against loan signing agents average around $14,000. Some companies may ask for an even larger insurance policy, so it's important to be aware of the requirements before agreeing to work with a new client. However, even a $25,000 policy can provide significant protection against damages resulting from unintentional mistakes.

While an E&O policy is not required by law, it can provide peace of mind and financial protection in the event of a mistake. In addition, most E&O policies also cover legal expenses, which can be invaluable if you are sued. As a result, carrying an E&O policy is generally considered to be a wise investment for any loan signing agent. There are several different companies that offer courses and exams for becoming a certified signing professional.

The Signing Professionals Workgroup oversees the certification process and sets the standards for courses and exams. Many lenders, title companies, and signing services require certification from the SPW, so taking a course that is approved by the SPW can help you to qualify for more jobs. As a result, it is generally advisable to choose a course and exam from an SPW-compliant company in order to ensure that you will meet the requirements of most employers.

As a loan signing agent, you are given access to borrowers' private financial information. In order to protect this sensitive data, the certification process includes a background check. This allows certification organizations to confirm that the individual has no criminal history that would suggest they may be inclined to misuse this sensitive information.

The background check is an important part of the certification process, and it helps to safeguard borrowers' private data. This requirement helps to protect borrowers' information and maintain the integrity of the certification process.

<u>Steps to becoming a certified signing agent:</u>

In order to become a certified loan signing agent, you must first be a Notary Public in your state. Once you have done this, you then take a loan signing training course. After completing the course and passing the associated exam, you will need to undergo a background screening that is compliant with the Standards for Professional Notaries (SPW). You will also need to purchase your signing agent supplies and a minimum

$25,000 Errors and Omissions (E&O) insurance policy.

The purpose of the loan signing agent exam is to ensure that you have the knowledge and skills necessary to correctly and efficiently complete mortgage loan closings and other types of financial transactions. The exam covers both federal and state laws governing loan closings, as well as specific procedures that vary from state to state. In addition, the exam tests applicants' knowledge of notary laws and their ability to notarize documents properly. By successfully completing the exam, you will be able to show potential clients that you have the knowledge and skills necessary to help them navigate the complex world of financial transactions. Those who successfully pass the exam will be able to list themselves as certified loan signing agents with the National Notary Association. The loan signing agent exam is an open-book test that covers all topics related to the loan signing process. The National Notary Association offers a self-study guide that can be used during the exam. This guide covers all of the topics included in the exam and includes practice questions to help you prepare. This guide can be used during the exam and contains practice questions to help you prepare. In addition, there are several other resources available that will help you study for the exam, including practice exams and self-study guides. With preparation, you can confidently take the loan signing agent exam and start your new career.

After you purchase a course and exam package online, you will get an email with instructions on accessing the course and the exam. The email will contain a link to the course, and you will be able to take the exam online. Once you have submitted your answers, you will receive a pass/fail notification immediately. Plus, you'll have the ability to retake the exam if you don't pass it the first time. Once you pass the exam, you can then download and print your certificate of completion.

Joining a notary association has many advantages. One of the main benefits is the ability to connect with potential customers. Being connected with potential customers is a great advantage because it gives you the opportunity to build your clientele. Another benefit of joining an association is that you will be able to display a badge on your website or business card, which will demonstrate to potential customers that you are a member of a reputable organization. Finally, most associations have an active community of members who can provide support and share ideas. Joining a notary association is an important way to stay up-to-date on best practices and changes in the industry. The Notary Association of America (NAA) and National Notary (NNA) are two well-respected organizations that offer annual memberships. Annual membership with NAA starts at $39, while annual membership with NNA starts at $69. Both organizations offer a variety of benefits, including discounts on education and supplies, access to a community of notaries, and monthly updates on the latest industry news. While the cost of membership may seem like a small expense, it can pay off in peace of mind and professional development.

Loan signing agents are a vital part of the mortgage industry, helping to ensure that documents are properly signed and notarized. While the government does not define a specific time frame for renewing your certification, the industry standard is to renew your exam and background check every year. This ensures that you are up-to-date on the latest procedures and that your skills are sharp. By renewing your loan signing agent certification on a yearly basis, you can ensure that you are providing the best possible service to your clients.

If you are enjoying reading this book so far, please take a second to leave a positive five-star review on Amazon. It means a lot knowing that you found this information helpful and encourages us to publish more notary books in the future.

Thank you for reading!

5

WORKING AS A NOTARY (STATE-BY-STATE REQUIREMENTS, TERMS, AND AUTHORIZED DUTIES)

I t is essential to understand the specific requirements set by your state before you apply to become a notary. By fulfilling all the requirements, you can ensure that you are qualified and prepared to serve the public as a notary. Every state requires that notaries be at least 18 years of age in the United States. In Nebraska, this age requirement is raised to 19. All other requirements for becoming a notary are set at the state level, hence the need for this chapter.

This chapter continues our look at the state-by-state requirements for becoming commissioned as a notary. **The requirements for exams and courses were detailed in the previous chapter.** The first part of this chapter looks at the other **relevant requirements to become commissioned as a notary** in each state. The second part looks at the **responsibilities of a notary** after receiving a commission, including requirements for keeping and updating a notary record book or journal, the use of an ink stamp, embossing seal, and electronic seal, any bonds legally required, and the term of office for a notary in each state. The third part of this chapter details the **authorized duties** prescribed to a notary, which can vary significantly from state to state.

Chances are, you only want the information for your one state, rendering the rest of the chapter useless - so the best thing to do will be to skip ahead to your state. **We've listed each one in alphabetical order** so that you can easily find your state, no matter whether you're listening to the audiobook or reading the paperback edition.

As a notary public, you have the vital task of ensuring that legal documents are executed and recorded properly. In order to do this, you must be familiar with the notary record book and journal requirements, ink stamp and embossing seal requirements, bond requirements, and terms of office for each state in which you practice. In every state in the US, notaries are authorized to administer oaths and affirmations. This means that they can swear in witnesses for depositions and trials, and take sworn statements. In addition, notaries are authorized to take acknowledgments of documents. This includes proofing the identity of signers, taking signatures, and administering oaths or affirmations, if required. Lastly, notaries in every state plus Washington D.C. are authorized to administer acknowledgments for deeds, mortgage documents, and powers of attorney.

What follows is a summary of the authorized duties of a commissioned notary in all fifty states plus Washington, DC. **We will endeavor to create updated editions of this section**, but we can only do this every so often. Therefore, to remain confident, you should contact your local Secretary of State's office and view their website, or go to https://www.asnnotary.org/?form=stateinfo for an updated list of requirements.

In **Alabama**, the notary requirements vary from county to county. There is no uniform set of requirements that all counties must follow, so applicants should check with their local county clerk's office to determine the specific requirements. Although the requirements may differ from county to county, all applicants must be at least 18 years of age. **Alabama** notaries are required to have a bond of $25,000. They are also required to use an ink stamp or embossing seal. Notaries in Alabama have a four-year term of office. As a commissioned notary in **Alabama**, you are authorized to administer oaths and affirmations, take acknowledgments and proofs, and make certified copies of register entries. Additionally, you are allowed to execute protests.

In **Alaska**, notaries must be residents of the state. They must also be legally in the country and have not had any felonies in the past 10 years or been incarcerated for a felony in the past 10 years. A small number of notary commissions are available, only to Federal, State, and Municipal employees. Notaries in **Alaska** are not required to use a record book or journal, except in the case of Remote Online Notaries. However, they are required to use an ink stamp or embossing seal. The stamp must be photographically reproducible, meaning that it can be easily copied. Notaries in Alaska are also required to have a bond of $2,500. Finally, notaries in this state have a four-year term of office, except for Limited Governmental Notaries whose term ends when they leave their government position. Notaries in **Alaska** are authorized to administer oaths and affirmations, acknowledgments, proofs, and to state that a tangible document is an accurate copy of an electronic document. Governmental notaries are prohibited from notarizing for the public.

In **Arizona**, notaries must be residents of the state and must be able to read and write English. They must also either be a US citizen or, alternatively, be legal permanent residents. Notaries must not have been convicted of a felony. If convicted of a felony, they must since have had their civil rights restored. Notaries also must not have been convicted of an offense related to moral turpitude. If you want to be a notary in **Arizona**, you are required to use a paper journal for public records and another for non-public records. Additionally, remote online notarizations must be recorded in an electronic journal, along with an audiovisual recording of the notarization. They must also use an ink stamp for paper notarial acts and an embossing seal only in conjunction with the official ink stamp. Electronic and remote online notarizations must include a notary's electronic seal. Notaries are required to have a bond of $5,000 and will be commissioned for a four-year term of office. A notary in **Arizona** is authorized to administer oaths and affirmations, acknowledgments and proofs, and attest to copies.

In **Arkansas**, out-of-state applicants are permissible in certain circumstances. All individuals applying must understand how to read and write in English, and must either be a US citizen or legal permanent resident. In addition, applicants must not have had a notary commission revoked over the past 10 years and can't have any felonies. In **Arkansas**, notaries are not required to use a recordbook or journal, but they are required to use an ink stamp or embossing seal, which must be photographically reproducible. An electronic seal is specified for electronic and remote online notarizations. In Arkansas, notaries are required to have a bond of $7,500. A notary's term of office is 10 years. Notaries in **Arkansas** are authorized to administer oaths and affirmations, acknowledgments and proofs, take affidavits and depositions and swear-in witnesses, attest to copies, and execute protests.

In **California**, all notaries must be residents of the state. Furthermore, they must not fall into any of the state's disqualification categories. In **California**, notaries are required to maintain a recordbook for both paper and electronic notarizations. They are also required to take thumbprints for instruments affecting real property and for powers of attorney. In addition, notaries in California are required to use an ink stamp or embossing seal. The stamp must be photographically reproducible. There is also an electronic seal specified for electronic and remote online notarizations. Lastly, in California, notaries are required to have a bond of $15,000 and a 4-year term of office. A notary in **California** is authorized to administer oaths and affirmations, acknowledgments, proofs, and take affidavits and depositions and swear-in witnesses. They can also attest to copies of notarial recordbook entries and powers of attorney, execute protests (only if employed by a financial institution), and perform other related duties.

In **Colorado**, all notaries must be residents of or employed within the state. Similar to Arkansas and California, applicants must either be a US citizen/permanent resident and must be able to read and write English. Additionally, they must not fall into any of the state's disqualification categories. In **Colorado**, notaries are required to maintain a recordbook for paper and electronic notarizations. Remote online notarizations have to be recorded in an electronic journal, along with an audiovisual recording of the notarization. Notaries are not required to use a notary seal, and a bond is not required. Colorado notaries enjoy a 4-year term of office. A commissioned notary in **Colorado** is authorized to administer oaths and affirmations, acknowledgments and proofs, attest to copies, witness signatures, take affidavits and depositions and swear-in witnesses, and execute protests.

In **Connecticut**, notaries are required to be residents of or employed within the state. Non-residents must provide their employment address to the state and must provide their email address to receive correspondence. In **Connecticut**, a notary recordbook or journal is not required. Similarly, notaries are not required to use a notary seal. A bond is also not required. Finally, notaries in Connecticut have a 5-year term of office. Notaries in **Connecticut** are authorized to administer oaths and affirmations, acknowledgments and proofs, take depositions, issue subpoenas for a specified purpose, and attest to copies.

A notary public in **Delaware** is required to be a resident of the state or employed within the state. Non-residents must provide their employment address to the state and must have a reasonable need for a notary commission. Notaries must also be of good character and, if they were convicted of a felony, must have had their civil rights restored. Notary commissions are only available to State employees, while Service Organization Notary commissions are available in limited circumstances. In **Delaware**, a notary recordbook or journal is not required for paper notarial acts but is required for electronic notarial acts. Notaries are required to use an ink stamp or embossing seal for paper notarial acts. The ink stamp must be photographically reproducible. An electronic seal is specified for electronic and remote online notarizations, but a bond is not required. Traditional notaries and electronic notaries in Delaware have a 2-year term of office, while service organization notaries have a 4-year term of office. Limited Governmental Notaries maintain their position for as long as they stay employed by the government agency. A commissioned notary in **Delaware** is authorized to administer oaths and affirmations, acknowledgments and proofs, witness signatures, attest to copies, and execute protests. Governmental notaries are not permitted to notarize for the public.

Florida notaries must be a resident of the state, able to read, write, and understand English, and have had their civil rights restored if they have been convicted of a felony. In **Florida**, a notary is not required to have a recordbook or journal when the principal is physically present. Remote online notarizations must be recorded in an electronic journal, along with an audiovisual recording of the notarization. Notaries are requried to use a round or rectangular ink stamp for paper notarial acts, and an embossing seal can only be used alongside the official ink stamp. The ink stamp must be photographically reproducible. For electronic notarizations, a notary may use their electronic signature provided it contains the same information as the ink stamp. Notaries in Florida must take out a bond of $7,500, while Florida's Remote Online Notaries are required to have a bond of $25,000. Notaries have a 4-year term of office. A notary in **Florida** is authorized to administer oaths and affirmations, acknowledgments and proofs, attest to copies of certain documents, perform marriage ceremonies, verify vehicle identification numbers, certify the contents of safe deposit boxes, execute protests, and state that a tangible document is an accurate copy of an electronic document.

A notary public in **Georgia** is required to be a US citizen or permanent resident, should read and write English, and provide their phone number. They must also reside in or be employed within the county in which they are applying. In the state of **Georgia**, a notary is not required to keep a recordbook or journal detailing their notarial acts. However, they are required by law to use an ink stamp or embossing seal for all paper notarial acts. Notaries in Georgia do not have to post a bond, and their term of office is four years. A notary in the state of **Georgia** is authorized to administer oaths and affirmations, acknowledgments, and proofs, as well as to certify and attest to copies.

They are also authorized to witness affidavits and signatures.

A notary public in **Hawaii** must be a resident of the state, a United States citizen, and possess the qualifications required of public officers. Yes, in **Hawaii**, a paper journal is required that must conform to specific requirements. Notaries are required to use a round ink stamp for paper notarial acts and must hold a bond of $1,000. Notaries in Hawaii have a 4-year term of office. A notary in **Hawaii** is authorized to administer oaths and affirmations, acknowledgments and proofs, witness signatures and attest to the identity of a document signer, execute protests, and take depositions.

Idaho notaries must be residents of or employed within the state, US citizens or legal permanent residents, able to read and write English, and not fall into any of the state's disqualification categories. In Idaho, **notaries** are required to keep a notary recordbook or journal, but an audiovisual recording of remote online notarizations must be kept. Notaries must use an ink stamp for paper notarial acts, with an official stamp being required for electronic and remote online notarizations. In addition, notaries in Idaho are required to have a bond of $10,000 or the functional equivalent. The term of office for a notary in Idaho is six years. A notary in **Idaho** is authorized to administer oaths and affirmations, certify copies, witness and attest to signatures, note and execute protests, and state that a tangible document is an accurate replica of an electronic document.

In addition to being a resident of or employed within the state for at least 30 days, a notary in **Illinois** must also be a US citizen or a permanent resident. They must also be able to read and write English and can't have any felonies or have had a notary commission suspended/revoked in the past 10 years. In order to become a notary in **Illinois**, you must hold a $5,000 bond. You are required to use an ink stamp for paper notarial acts, which must be photographically reproducible, but you don't need to maintain a recordbook or journal. Resident notaries have a 4-year term of office, while non-resident notaries have a 1-year term of office. A commissioned notary in **Illinois** is authorized to administer oaths and affirmations, acknowledgments, proofs of execution, and witness signatures.

A notary public in **Indiana** must be a resident of or employed within the state. They must also not fall into any of the state's disqualification categories, have been convicted of an offense involving deceit, dishonesty, or fraud, or have a conviction where the sentence imposed was longer than 6 months. In **Indiana**, a notary recordbook or journal is not required except for Remote Online Notaries, in which case an electronic journal and audiovisual recording of the notarization must be kept. All parties must be informed about the recording prior to the notarial act. Notaries are also required to use an ink stamp for paper notarial acts, which must be photographically reproducible. In Indiana, the bond for notaries is $25,000 or the functional equivalent. The term of office for notaries in Indiana is 8 years. A commissioned notary in **Indiana** is authorized to administer oaths and affirmations, acknowledgments and proofs, as well as witness signatures, attest to copies, state that a tangible document is an accurate version of an electronic document, and execute protests.

A notary public in **Iowa** is required to be a resident of or employed within the state. They must also be a US citizen/legal permanent resident and be able to read and write English. Notaries in Iowa are also prohibited from engaging in certain activities. In **Iowa**, there are no specific requirements for notaries regarding the use of a recordbook or journal, except for those engaged in remote online notarizations for which an audiovisual recording of the notarization process must be kept. For paper notarial acts, Iowa notaries must use an official ink stamp or embossing seal, which must be photographically reproducible. An electronic stamp is allowed but not required for electronic and remote online notarizations. Notaries in Iowa are not required to post a bond. Resident notaries have a 3-year term of office, while non-resident notaries have a 1-year term. A notary in **Iowa** is authorized to administer oaths and affirmations, acknowledgments and proofs, certify copies, and note or execute protests. They can also witness and attest to signatures.

Kansas law requires that notaries be residents of or employed in the state. This ensures that notaries are familiar with Kansas law and are qualified to notarize documents within the state. Notaries in **Kansas** must maintain a journal with each of their notarial acts and must have a bond of $12,000. You will also need to purchase and use a notary stamp that is photographically reproducible and an electronic seal for electronic and remote online notarizations. Their term of office is four years. A commissioned notary in **Kansas** is authorized to witness signatures, attest to copies, and execute protests. In addition, they may administer oaths and affirmations, acknowledgments, and proofs.

Kentucky notaries are required to be residents of the state or employed within the county in which they are applying. They must also be US citizens or legal permanent residents and be able to read and write English. Additionally, Kentucky notaries cannot fall into any of the state's disqualification categories. Notaries in **Kentucky** are not required to keep a notary journal or recordbook, although all remote online notarizations must be recorded in an electronic journal along with an audiovisual recording of the notarization. You are not required to use a notary seal, but if you do choose to use one, you must follow certain statutory rules. You will also need to purchase a surety bond of $1,000. Once you have been appointed, you will have a four-year term of office. A notary public in **Kentucky** is authorized to administer oaths and affirmations, acknowledgments, proofs of execution, and to perform other notarial acts. They are also authorized to witness and attest to signatures, certify copies, certify depositions of witnesses, note and execute protests, and state that a tangible document is an accurate copy of an electronic document.

Do you want to work as a notary in **Louisiana**? You have to be a US citizen/legal permanent resident, be registered to vote in the parish in which you are applying, be able to read, write and speak English, and have not been convicted or pardoned of a felony. In addition, you must hold certain educational qualifications. In **Louisiana**, public notaries are required to keep a record book or journal of all notarizations involving immovable property. Remote online notarizations must also be recorded in an electronic journal, along with an audiovisual recording of the notarization. Notaries are not required to use a notary seal, as the Notary's signature itself is considered to be the notarial seal. Notaries are required to have a bond of $10,000 and errors and omissions insurance; however, attorneys are exempt from the insurance requirement. In Louisiana, notaries enjoy a lifetime commission. A notary in **Louisiana** is authorized to administer oaths and affirmations, acknowledgments and proofs, as well as attest to copies, undertake the specific tasks listed in Louisiana Revised Statutes 35:2, and state that a tangible document is an accurate reproduction of an electronic document.

If you are interested in becoming a notary, **Maine** has some requirements that you must meet. First, you must be a resident of or employed within the state. You must also demonstrate good proficiency in the English language. Additionally, you must be recommended for a notary commission by a registered voter in the state. Finally, you cannot have had your notary commission revoked over the past 5 years, nor have you been convicted of and imprisoned for a felony. You cannot have also been convicted of an offense involving dishonesty in the past 10 years. In **Maine**, a notary is not required to use a notary seal, but if you choose to do so, you must follow certain statutory rules. A notary recordbook or journal is only required for marriage ceremonies. Notaries are prohibited from collecting a thumbprint for any reason. A bond is also not required for Maine notaries. Lastly, Maine resident notaries have a 7-year term of office, while New Hampshire resident notaries only have a 4-year term in office. Notaries in **Maine** are authorized to administer oaths and affirmations, acknowledgments and proofs, attest documents, perform marriage ceremonies, and execute protests. It is recommended that a sworn affidavit as to a copy's authenticity be executed before a notary since the law is silent as to whether a notary may certify copies of original documents.

In order to become a notary in **Maryland**, you must be a resident of or employed within the state. You must also be of good character, integrity, and abilities. A **Maryland** notary is required to maintain a record-book, also known as a fair register. For remote online notarizations, an audiovisual recording of the notarization process must be kept. Additionally, notaries are required to use an ink stamp or embossing seal for paper notarial acts. However, an electronic stamp is allowed but not required for electronic and remote online notarizations. A bond is not required in Maryland. Finally, notaries have a four-year term of office. A notary in **Maryland** is authorized to administer oaths and affirmations, acknowledgments and proofs, attest to copies, witness signatures, execute protests, and state that a tangible document is an accurate copy of an electronic document.

If you want to be a notary in **Massachusetts**, you must be a resident of the state or regularly conduct business in the state. Once you are sworn in as a **Massachusetts** notary, you will be given a commission that is valid for seven years. A bond is not required. During your term of office, you are required to maintain a journal with each notarial act performed, and you must use an official ink stamp or embossing seal for paper notarial acts. It is permissible to use an embossing seal, but only in conjunction with the ink stamp. Attorneys and notaries who are employed by an attorney or the government are exempt from the journal requirement. A commissioned notary in **Massachusetts** is authorized to witness signatures, administer oaths and affirmations, acknowledgments and proofs, as well as attest to copies, issue summonses for witnesses, issue subpoenas, and witness the opening of bank safes, vaults, or boxes.

If you want to be a notary in **Michigan**, you must reside in or maintain a place of business in the state, know how to read and write English, be a US citizen or legal permanent resident, reside or be employed within the county in which you are applying, and have not been convicted of a felony in the past 10 years or a prescribed number of misdemeanor offenses. In **Michigan**, a notary is not required to have a record-book or journal, except for Remote Online Notaries, who must also keep an audiovisual recording of the notarization. Notaries are not required to use a notary seal; however, if a seal is used, it must be photographically reproducible and not cause anything on the document to be made illegible. An embossing seal can only be used alongside the official ink stamp. In Michigan, notaries are required to have a bond of $10,000 and have a 6 to a 7-year term of office. A notary in **Michigan** is authorized to administer oaths and affirmations, acknowledgments and proofs, and witness signatures. Notably, Michigan notaries are prohibited from stating that a tangible document is an accurate copy of an electronic document.

If you're in Minnesota, there aren't many require-ments. You simply must be a resident of the state or a bordering state, and you must be at least 18 years old.

To become a notary in **Minnesota**, notaries are required to use a photographically reproducible rectangular ink stamp for paper notarial acts. An embossing seal can only be used alongside the official ink stamp. For electronic notarizations where the individual is physically present, an electronic stamp is allowed but not required. If the individual is not physically present, an electronic seal must be used for electronic and remote online notarizations. A bond is not required to become a notary in Minnesota. Notaries have a 5-year term of office. A commissioned notary in **Minnesota** is authorized to administer oaths and affirmations, acknowledgments and proofs, witness signatures, attest to copies, state that a tangible document is an accurate reproduction of an electronic document, and execute protests, but only of a negotiable instrument.

If you would like to be a notary in **Mississippi**, you must meet the following requirements: be a resident of the state and reside in the county for at least 30 days, be a US citizen or legal permanent resident, know how to read and write English, and not have been convicted of a felony unless you have been pardoned. You must also not be incarcerated, on probation, or on parole. To be a notary in **Mississippi**, you must maintain a recordbook for paper and electronic notarizations in a paper journal that conforms to specific requirements. You must also use a circular ink stamp for paper notarial acts, which must be sharp, legible, permanent, and photographically reproducible. You may only use an embossing seal in conjunction with the official ink stamp and under certain circumstances. A Mississippi notary must have a $5,000 surety bond and will enjoy a term of office of 4 years. A notary in **Mississippi** is authorized to administer oaths and affirmations, acknowledgments, proofs, and witness signatures.

If you wish to work as a notary public in **the state of Missouri**, you must meet the following requirements: reside in the county in which you are applying, know how to read and write in English, be registered to vote in the county or be a legal permanent resident, and have not had your notary commission suspended in the past 10 years. Non-residents may apply for a notary commission under limited circumstances. In **Missouri**, notaries are required to maintain a record-book for paper and electronic notarizations in a paper journal that must conform to specific requirements. They must also keep a separate electronic journal of electronic notarial acts. Notaries are also required to use an ink stamp for paper notarial acts, which must be sharp, legible, permanent, and photographically reproducible. An embossing seal can only be used alongside the official ink stamp and under certain circumstances. An electronic seal is specified for electronic and remote online notarizations. Notaries need a bond of $10,000 and have a 4-year term of office. Notaries in **Missouri** are authorized to perform a variety of duties, including administering oaths and affirmations, acknowledgments, and proofs. They are also authorized to witness and attest signatures, as well as state that a tangible document is an accurate reproduction of an electronic document.

If you intend on becoming a notary in the state of **Montana**, you must be a US citizen or a permanent resident. Out-of-state applicants are permissible in certain circumstances, but all applicants have to read and write English. In **Montana**, notaries are required to maintain a paper or electronic recordbook for all paper and electronic notarizations, and an audiovisual recording of the notarization must be kept for remote online notarizations. Notaries are required to use an ink stamp for paper notarial acts and an electronic seal for electronic and remote online notarizations. The electronic seal must have the same appearance as the ink stamp. Notaries are required to have a bond of $25,000 and have a 4-year term of office. A notary in **Montana** is authorized to administer oaths and affirmations, acknowledgments and proofs, witness signatures, state that a tangible document is an accurate reproduction of an electronic document, execute protests, certify the transcripts of depositions or affidavits, and perform certifications of a fact or event. They are also authorized to perform marriage ceremonies.

In **Nebraska**, notaries must reside in or be employed within the state and must not have been convicted of any offenses involving dishonesty or fraud in the past 5 years. In **Nebraska**, notaries must keep a record of all paper and electronic notarizations in an electronic recordbook. In addition, an audiovisual recording must be made and kept for all remote online notarizations. Notaries in Nebraska must use an ink stamp for paper notarizations and an electronic seal for electronic and remote online notarizations. Notaries must hold a $15,000 bond and will be given a term of four years. **Nebraska** notaries are authorized to administer oaths and affirmations, acknowledgments and proofs, take depositions, attest documents, issue summonses for witnesses, execute protests, and witness signatures, including for those physically unable to sign.

In **Nevada**, notaries must be residents of the state and possess their civil rights. Out-of-state applicants are permissible in certain circumstances. To work as a notary in **Nevada**, you must use a paper journal that conforms to specific requirements for all notarizations. You must also keep a separate electronic journal to record electronic notarial acts. For remote online notarizations, you must keep an audiovisual recording of the notarization but ensure that all parties are informed about the recording prior to the notarial act. Notaries are required to use a photographically reproducible ink stamp with indelible ink for paper notarial acts, while a mechanical stamp is required for electronic and remote online notarizations. This includes imprints made by a computer or other device. A

$10,000 bond is required, and notaries have a 4-year term of office. A commissioned notary in **Nevada** is authorized to administer oaths and affirmations, acknowledgments and proofs, and attest to copies. They can also execute protests provided that doing so is within the scope of their employment with a depository institution. Nevada notaries are permitted to perform marriage ceremonies after obtaining a certificate from a county clerk.

In order to become a notary public in **New Hampshire**, you must be a resident of the state or a bordering state, and you can not have been convicted of a felony unless it has been annulled or unless it was a minor traffic violation. You must also be endorsed for a notary commission by two notaries and one registered voter of the state, and you must complete a Criminal Record Release Authorization Form. In **New Hampshire**, a notary is not required to have a record-book or journal, nor are they required to have a bond. However, they are required to use an ink stamp or embossing seal for paper notarial acts. The term of office for a New Hampshire notary is 5 years. Commissioned notaries in **New Hampshire** are authorized to administer oaths and affirmations, acknowledgments and proofs, witness signatures, attest to copies, witness the opening of bank safe deposit boxes, take depositions, and execute protests.

In order to become a notary public in **New Jersey**, you must be a resident of the state or a bordering state with regular employment in the state, and you cannot have been convicted of an offense related to dishonesty or any crime of the first or second degree. In **New Jersey**, most notaries must record all paper and electronic notarizations in either an electronic or paper recordbook. However, certain categories of notaries are exempt from this requirement. All notaries are required to use a photographically reproducible ink stamp for paper notarizations. A bond is not required, and a New Jersey notary will hold their office for five years. A commissioned notary in **New Jersey** can administer oaths and affirmations, acknowledgments and proofs, witness signatures, certify the contents of safe deposit boxes, attest to copies, take depositions, and state that a tangible document is an accurate copy of an electronic document. They can also execute protests.

If you would like to be a notary in the state of **New Mexico**, you must be a resident of the state and understand how to read and write in English. You must not have been convicted of any felonies, not have pleaded guilty or no contest to a felony, and have not had your notary commission revoked in the past 5 years. In order to become a notary in **New Mexico**, you must have a bond of $10,000 and maintain both a paper and electronic recordbook for paper and electronic notarizations, respectively. You must also use a photographically reproducible ink stamp with permanent ink or an embossing seal for paper notarial acts.

Notaries in New Mexico have a 4-year term of office. A **New Mexico** notary is authorized to administer oaths and affirmations, acknowledgments, and proofs, as well as certify and attest to copies and signatures. They are also authorized to note and execute protests under limited circumstances and state that a tangible document is an accurate copy of an electronic document.

If you want to be a notary in **New York**, you must reside in or be employed within the state. You must also be of 'good character' and must either be a US citizen or a legal permanent resident. You must hold certain educational qualifications, and you can not have been convicted of a felony or certain misdemeanors. **New York** notaries are not required to maintain a notary recordbook or journal, use a notary seal, or post a bond. Their term of office is four years. A commissioned notary in **New York** is authorized to administer oaths and affirmations, acknowledgments and proofs, take depositions, witness affidavits, and execute protests.

If you're interested in working as a notary in **North Carolina**, you'll need to be a resident of or employed within the state. You'll also need to read, write, and speak English and be legally in the United States. Additionally, you must hold certain educational qualifications and possess the relevant approved manual. Finally, you cannot fall into any of North Carolina's disqualification categories. In **North Carolina**, a notary recordbook or journal is not required for paper notarizations. However, the Secretary of State has the discretion to require electronic notarizations to be recorded. Notaries are required to use an ink stamp or embossing seal for paper notarial acts. The ink stamp must be photographically reproducible. An electronic seal that must replicate the appearance of the ink seal is specified for electronic and remote online notarizations. In North Carolina, a bond is not required, and notaries have a 5-year term of office. A notary in **North Carolina** is authorized to administer oaths and affirmations, acknowledgments, and proofs. In addition, they are authorized to take an oath or affirmation from a witness to another person's signature under limited circumstances.

In order to become a notary in **North Dakota**, you must be a resident of the state, read and write English, and be either a US citizen or permanent resident. Applicants from out-of-state can apply to become a notary under certain circumstances. In order to become a notary in **North Dakota**, you must maintain either a paper or electronic recordbook for all remote notarizations, you must keep an audiovisual notarization recording for all remote online notarizations, you must use a photographically reproducible ink stamp for all paper notarial acts, and you cannot use an embosser. Note that an electronic stamp is not required for electronic and remote online notarizations, provided the notarial certificate contains specified information. Provided you have a bond of $7,500; you will receive a 4-year term of office. A commissioned notary in **North Dakota** is authorized to administer oaths and affirmations, acknowledgments and proofs, witness signatures, attest to copies, execute protests, and state that a tangible document is an accurate reproduction of an electronic document. They are restrained by section 44-06.1-23 of the North Dakota Century Code.

In **Ohio**, notaries must also be residents of the state and meet all other requirements, including not having been convicted of certain offenses or pleaded guilty or no contest to a felony. Out-of-state applicants may be accepted under certain circumstances. In the state of **Ohio**, all remote online notarizations must be recorded in an electronic journal, along with an audio-visual recording of the notarization. Notaries are required to use an ink stamp or embossing seal for paper notarial acts and an electronic seal for electronic and remote online notarizations. A bond is not required, and notaries have a 5-year term of office. In addition to administering oaths and affirmations, acknowledgments, and proofs, notaries in Ohio are also authorized to take and certify depositions.

In **Oklahoma**, notaries must be residents of the state or a bordering state with regular employment in Oklahoma, know how to read and write in English, and have no felony convictions. In order to work as a notary in the state of **Oklahoma**, a notary recordbook or journal must be maintained for the notarization of absentee ballot affidavits and protests noted for banks. For all other paper notarization acts, a record is not required. Remote online notarizations must be recorded in an electronic journal along with an audio-visual recording of the notarization. Notaries are required to use an ink stamp or embossing seal for paper notarial acts and an electronic seal for electronic and remote online notarizations. Oklahoma notaries are required to have a bond of $1,000 and will have a 4-year term of office. A notary in **Oklahoma** is authorized to administer oaths and affirmations, acknowledgments, and proofs, as well as attest to copies and signatures, execute protests, and state that a tangible document is an accurate copy of an electronic document.

In **Oregon**, notaries must reside in or be employed within the state and must know how to read and write in English. They must also not have had their notary commission revoked in the past 10 years or been convicted of an offense involving deceit, dishonesty, or fraud in the past 10 years. They must also not fall into any of Oregon's disqualification categories. In **Oregon**, notaries are required to maintain either a paper or electronic recordbook for all notarizations, whether paper or electronic. They are also required to use an ink stamp for paper notarial acts, which must be legible and photographically reproducible. An embossing seal can only be used along with the official ink stamp. For electronic notarizations, an electronic stamp is optional, provided the notarial certificate contains specified information. In Oregon, a bond is not required, and notaries have a 4-year term of office. **Oregon** notaries are authorized to administer oaths and affirmations, acknowledgments and proofs, and witness signatures. They are also authorized to attest to copies and execute protests under limited circumstances.

In **Pennsylvania**, notaries must reside in or be employed within the state and either be US citizens or legal permanent residents. They must also know how to read and write English and not fall into any of the state's disqualification categories. In **Pennsylvania**, notaries are required to maintain either a paper or electronic recordbook for all paper and electronic notarizations. Notaries are also required to use an ink stamp for paper notarial acts, and the ink stamp must be photographically reproducible. An embossing seal can only be used along with the official ink stamp. An electronic stamp is optional for electronic notarizations, provided the notarial certificate contains specified information. If a notary chooses to use an electronic stamp, they must follow certain statutory rules. Pennsylvania notaries are required to have a bond of $10,000 and will have a 4-year term of office. **Pennsylvania** notaries are authorized to administer oaths and affirmations, acknowledgments, and proofs, as well as attest to copies and signatures, certify depositions of witnesses, and execute protests.

Becoming a notary in **Rhode Island** involves the following steps. First, you must be a resident of or employed within the state. You must also be a US citizen/legal permanent resident, and you must know how to read and write in English. Finally, you must not fall into any of the state's disqualification categories, and you must demonstrate good knowledge of the powers and duties of a Notary public. In **Rhode Island**, a notary is not required to have a recordbook or journal. However, they are required to use an ink stamp for paper notarial acts, and their notary certificates must include their seal. An electronic seal is specified for electronic and remote online notarizations. Notaries in Rhode Island do not have to post a bond. Their term of office is four years. A commissioned notary in **Rhode Island** is authorized to administer oaths, affirmations, acknowledgments and proofs, witness signatures, certify copies, issue subpoenas and depose witnesses (if they have specific expertise), and execute protests.

If you intend to become a notary in **South Carolina**, you must first be registered to vote and be able to read and write English. You must also submit an application that is true and complete. As a notary in **South Carolina**, you are required to maintain a journal of your notarial acts and are strongly encouraged to use an ink stamp or embossing seal for paper notarial acts.

You must also include your official title under your signature on the notarial certificate. South Carolina notaries are issued a commission that is valid for 10 years. A bond is not required. A commissioned notary in **South Carolina** is authorized to administer oaths and affirmations, acknowledgments, and proofs, as well as execute signature witnessing and protests and perform marriage ceremonies.

Notaries public in **South Dakota** must be a resident of the state or a bordering state with regular employment in the state. They must also not have been convicted of a felony. In **South Dakota**, a notary is not required to have a recordbook or journal unless the person does not appear before the Notary in person or electronically. Notaries are required to use an ink stamp or embossing seal for paper notarial acts and must hold a bond of $5,000. The term of office for a notary in South Dakota is six years. A commissioned notary in **South Dakota** is authorized to administer oaths and affirmations, acknowledgments and proofs, witness signatures, attest to copies, and execute protests.

In order to become a notary in **Tennessee**, you must be a resident of or employed within the state, be a US citizen or legal permanent resident, not have had a notary commission revoked, and not fall into any of the state's disqualification categories. As a notary in **Tennessee**, you must have a notary recordbook or journal - unless you or your employer does not charge fees for notarial services. For remote online notarizations, you must have an audiovisual recording of the notarization in addition to a record in your electronic journal. Notaries in Tennessee are required to use a photographically reproducible round ink stamp for paper notarial acts; the ink color must not be yellow or black, but the stamp should appear black when photocopied. An official stamp is also required for electronic and remote online notarizations performed by a commissioned Tennessee Online Notary Public. All notaries in Tennessee must have a bond of $10,000. Notaries' terms of office are 4 years. As a commissioned notary in **Tennessee**, you are authorized to administer oaths and affirmations, acknowledgments and proofs, and to take affidavits and depositions.

In order to become a notary public in the state of **Texas**, you must be a resident of Texas and have not been convicted of any offenses involving moral turpitude, and have not been convicted of a felony. As a notary in **Texas**, you must maintain either a paper or electronic recordbook for all paper and electronic notarizations, while remote online notarizations must be recorded in an electronic journal. You must use an ink stamp or embossing seal (that is photographically reproducible and uses indelible ink) for paper notarial acts and have a $10,000 surety bond. Online notaries must use an X.509 digital certificate and an electronic seal. The term of office for a notary in Texas is four years. Notaries in **Texas** are authorized to attest to copies of certain documents, take depositions, execute protests, state that a tangible document is an accurate reproduction of an electronic document, and administer oaths and affirmations, acknowledgments, and proofs.

If you intend to become a notary in **Utah**, you must be a US citizen/legal resident and be able to read, write, and understand English. You must also have been a resident of the state for 30 days. During your term as a notary in **Utah**, you will only be required to record remote online notarizations in an electronic journal, along with an audiovisual recording. No record is required for paper notarizations. A photographically reproducible ink stamp with purple ink must be used for paper notarial acts. Embossing seals are permitted but can only be used in conjunction with the official ink stamp. Electronic and remote online notarizations require an electronic seal. All Utah notaries have a 4-year term of office. A $5,000 surety bond is required for general notaries, while Remote Online Notaries need a $10,000 bond. A notary in **Utah** is authorized to witness signatures, attest to copies, and administer oaths and affirmations, acknowledgments, and proofs.

In **Vermont**, notaries must reside in or be employed within the state. They must also be either US citizens or legal permanent residents. In **Vermont**, there is no requirement for a notary to maintain a recordbook or journal. Notaries are also not required to use a notary seal as long as their name, and commission number is clearly visible on the notarial certificate. However, if a notary chooses to use a seal, the image or embossment must be photographically reproducible. In Vermont, bonds are not required for notaries. Notaries in Vermont have a two-year term of office. A notary in **Vermont** is authorized to administer oaths and affirmations, acknowledgments and proofs, as well as witness signatures and execute protests.

In **Virginia**, a notary must be a resident of or employed within the state, be legally in the United States, know how to read and write English, and have had their civil rights restored if they have been convicted of a felony. In **Virginia**, paper notarial acts do not need to be recorded, while remote online notarizations have to be recorded in an electronic journal, along with an audiovisual recording of the notarization. Notaries are required to use an ink stamp or embossing seal for paper notarial acts. This stamp or seal must be sharp, legible, permanent, and photographically reproducible. For electronic and remote online notarizations, there is also an electronic seal specified under the eNotarization Assurance Standard. Notaries have a 4-year term of office. A notary in **Virginia** is authorized to administer oaths and affirmations, acknowledgments and proofs, as well as certify depositions and copies, and witness affidavits.

If you want to be a notary in **Washington** state, you must be a resident or be employed within the state. You must also be a US citizen or a legal permanent resident and be able to read and write in English. In the state of **Washington**, a paper journal is required for all notarizations. Additionally, an audiovisual recording of the notarization process must be kept on file for remote online notarizations. Notaries are also required to use an ink stamp or embossing seal for paper notarial acts, which must be indelible and photographically reproducible. Furthermore, an official stamp is required for electronic and remote online notarizations that provides a digital image likeness of the stamp shown on a paper notarization. All notaries in Washington are required to have a $10,000 bond and hold office for a four-year term. A commissioned notary in **Washington** is authorized to administer oaths and affirmations, acknowledgments and proofs, witness signatures, attest to copies, certify that an event has occurred or that an act has been performed, and state that a tangible document is an accurate copy of an electronic document. Subject to restrictions, they can also execute protests of a negotiable instrument.

Becoming a notary public in **Washington** DC requires being either a United States citizen or a legal permanent resident. In **Washington, DC**, notaries are required to maintain either a paper or electronic recordbook for all paper and electronic notarizations. The journal entry must be made contemporaneously with the notarial act. Notaries are required to use an embossing seal and seal impression inker for paper notarial acts, while an electronic seal is specified for electronic notarizations. In Washington, DC, notaries are required to have a bond of $2,000 or the functional equivalent. Notaries have a 5-year term of office. A notary in **Washington, DC,** is authorized to administer oaths and affirmations, acknowledgments and proofs, witness signatures, attest to copies of certain documents, and execute protests. Unlike regular notaries, governmental notaries in Washington, DC, are prohibited from notarizing for the public.

West Virginia notaries must be residents of the state or a bordering state with regular employment in West Virginia, US citizens or legal permanent residents, able to read and write English and hold certain educational qualifications. They must also not fall into any of the state's disqualification categories. In **West Virginia**, notaries aren't required to have a recordbook or journal, but if they choose to use an electronic journal, it must comply with the administrative rules of the Secretary of State. Notaries are required to use an ink stamp for paper notarial acts, with an embossing seal only to be used alongside the official ink stamp. An electronic notary seal is required for electronic notarizations. West Virginia notaries are not required to have a bond, and they have a 5-year term of office. A commissioned notary in **West Virginia** is authorized to administer oaths and affirmations, acknowledgments and proofs, witness signatures, attest to copies, and execute protests.

Wisconsin has certain requirements that you must meet. You have to be a permanent resident of the United States, hold certain educational qualifications, and adhere to Wisconsin notary laws. In **Wisconsin**, a notary recordbook or journal is not required for paper notarial acts, but an audiovisual notarization recording must be kept for remote online notarizations. Notaries are required to use a photographically reproducible ink stamp or embossing seal for paper notarial acts. Provided their name appears identically on each, notaries can choose to use both tools if desired. Notaries are not required to use an electronic stamp for electronic notarizations, provided the notarial certificate contains the necessary information. Notaries are required to have a bond of $500 and will have a 4-year term of office. **Wisconsin** commissioned notaries are authorized to administer oaths and affirmations, acknowledgments, and proofs, as well as to witness signatures, attest to copies, state that a tangible document is an accurate copy of an electronic document, take depositions, and execute protests.

Notaries in **Wyoming** must reside in or be employed within the state and must be either US citizens or otherwise legally in the country. They must also not fall into any of the state's disqualification categories. As of July 2021, **Wyoming** notaries are required to maintain a record book or journal. Notaries are also required to use a rectangular ink stamp for paper notarial acts. A bond is not required, and notaries have a 6-year term of office. A commissioned notary in **Wyoming** is authorized to witness signatures, attest to copies, and execute protests, but only of a negotiable instrument.

6

GETTING YOUR FIRST
CLIENTS & MARKETING
YOUR BUSINESS

Getting your first customer *seals* your entrance into the Notary business. More importantly, your first collection of customers helps test your business model and your understanding of the Notary industry. Lastly, operating with just one or two clients initially provides you with the flexibility to make changes and find the most effective approach.

Whether you plan to make your Notary business a side hustle or a primary source of income, the financial benefits are massively worthwhile. However, it's important to note that acquiring your first client(s) will require some effort like it would any other business. First, you must make people aware of your presence and then convince potential customers that you're reliable, secure, and worth their time with your presentation, offering, and communication.

These are strategies that hundreds of successful notaries have used to take their business from point A to B. Without any further ado, here's how to get your first client as a Notary:

1. Use the Internet

New businesses and side hustles pop up every day, with many offering and promising riches in a short period. This quick prosperity is often thanks to the internet since ad campaigns can now reach millions of people compared to traditional methods like mail or billboards that only engage thousands or hundreds. In other words, you have access to a larger base of potential clients, so building an online presence is essential. It also helps you look more professional and reliable since studies have shown that people research a product or brand online before dedicating their money and time.

Furthermore, you don't need to be a branding expert to capitalize on the internet since creating a credible online presence is simple and fast. Here are my recommendations:

- **Get a Website**

People question the legitimacy of a business without a website since the platform comforts people that you're a real business and makes a great first impression. Therefore, investing in a website increases your chances of getting your first client quickly. Furthermore, you don't need to learn web development or spend tens of thousands of dollars to have your brand's website up and running. Several easy platforms for building a website exist, including Wix.com, GoDaddy.com, and SiteBuilder.com. You can even include a Notary blog on your website, providing valuable information to people online. At the same time, blogging helps your website rank highly on search engines, gain more web traffic, and become more relevant in the Notary world.

- **Use Online Notary Directories**

Some clients prefer getting the safest and most reliable option, and instead of performing online research for qualified notaries, they opt for Notary directories. These websites list reliable notaries for people to assess and pick their desired professional, similar to platforms like Fiverr and Upwork.

Therefore, we recommend getting yourself and your business on these online Notary directories to increase your chances of popping up whenever people in your area search for a Notary. Some common Notary directories include *Bancserv.net, Exp Notary, Coast to Coast, Old Republic, and Amrock.** However, before signing up on these platforms, visit their website to understand whether their requirements are consistent with your goals. Also, note that most of these directories are either free or very low cost. Also, I recommend including additional information beyond your name and number; add elements like your experience, price, and additional contact information (website, email, LinkedIn, etc.). This is important since people can learn all they need to know about an expert before hiring them.

- **Use Social Media**

Social media platforms like Facebook, LinkedIn, Instagram, and Twitter receive billions of monthly impressions, making them perfect for building your brand & reaching out to potential clients. To begin creating a social media presence, pick one platform to focus on; dedicate time to growing your presence on that website - before moving to another one. For example, LinkedIn is a common social media recommendation for maximizing your Notary potential since the site is known for business-related purposes, not entertainment, like Instagram and Facebook.

- **Use PPC**

Once your website is up and you have a substantial social media presence, you can employ Pay-per-click advertising to drive more clients to your platforms. Pay-per-click advertising refers to ads appearing on the top of search engines or socials - and you pay a predetermined amount of money whenever someone clicks your link.

First, you research the keywords that best represent your Notary business in the search results. We recommend using more niche terms since bigger establishments might dominate you for clicks for more common terms. For example, instead of "Notary Public," try "professional Notary in Tallahassee, Florida ". Therefore, you should appear higher in the search results for a smaller cost-per-click. If your advertising budget is large, you can include multiple keywords to get clients faster. Multiple PPC service providers exist, but (Google) AdWords is the most popular due to its famous search engine.

- **Be Consistent**

Advertising your Notary business online is cost-effective, but results will not appear if you set up these profiles and leave. They need constant reassessment, tweaking, modifying, and maintenance. Therefore, we recommend staying consistent with your online marketing efforts.

2. Network

Famous business gurus like Robert Kiyosaki and Tim Ferris emphasize the importance of networking in every profession. Communicating and connecting with experts in your field and other areas is a cheat code for attaining financial prosperity. Therefore, prioritize reaching out to individuals and businesses most likely to require Notary services and let them know about your experience and dedication to delivering satisfaction. You should start by communicating with businesses and people in industries like real estate, health, law, car sales, and senior living facilities - among others. Also, dedicate time on your calendar to regularly communicate with these potential clients since frequent & non-intrusive communication raises your chances of being considered for Notary-related work.

3. Mention your Notary Services Frequently

There's nothing wrong with bringing up your profession whenever you're among adults who may need it. Essentially, whether you're at a family dinner, birthday party, or taking your child to soccer practice, let people know you're a notary. However, ensure that the subject flows naturally into the conversation, as injecting it forcefully into the conversation can be awkward or off-putting. While this strategy might not get you instant business, it keeps you in people's minds and sets you to receive their business whenever they require notary services.

4. Always Carry Marketing Materials

While going about your daily activities and informing people of your notary services, you can solidify your presence in their minds by leaving some marketing materials behind. You can leave business cards with people or drop fliers at venues like coffee shops or restaurants. You can take your marketing efforts a few steps further by giving out pens, hats, and shirts carrying your brand name, logo, and other identifiable elements. Irrespective of what marketing products you carry, ensure they carry your phone number, website URL, email address, areas of operation & availability hours, as well as additional services you offer.

5. Join a Local Organization

While you can join online Notary directories for better exposure to potential clients, you can do the same offline. Becoming a member of local organizations is a smart way to increase your credibility and attract more business to your brand. Some examples of these groups can include your local land title association or business networking groups. Upon having access to these professional gatherings, ensure to network, introduce yourself and sell your services to as many people as possible. Proper networking will raise your chances of employment, so capitalize on the activity. If communicating with the association's members seems intimidating, set a target to speak with a minimum of two potential clients per meeting, then raise the number when you feel more confident or at ease.

6. Join a Notary Association

Whether you wish to become a full-time Notary or perform the job as a side hustle, joining an association presents incredible benefits that reduce the stress of getting your first client. In addition, these organizations provide invaluable networking opportunities with relevant businesses and professional notaries. The live connection with other notaries allows you to ask questions, share opinions, receive criticism, and get guidance from experts with decades of experience. It's also worth noting that notaries can refer businesses to one another whenever they're too occupied to handle a job. Therefore, becoming a part of these Notary associations puts you in a position to get recommended to businesses or receive great advice for getting your first client. So it's worth the time and effort!

Once you've had your first few clients, here are some further marketing tips:

Follow Up on Previous Customers

Checking up on your clients weeks after they're done with your services is a good way to get repeat business or a happy recommendation. We recommend reaching out by sending a message or card thanking them for their patronage. Feel free to also ask for feedback or suggestions on how to improve your services. You can also capitalize on the holiday or season to send cards that show how much you care and also remind them of your business.

Experiment

Marketing isn't always straightforward; sometimes, you'll need to tweak your strategy to find the best way to connect with your audience. Therefore, we recommend staying on your toes and keep trying new marketing methods until you find the most effective method. You can assess your competitors or other successful notary businesses outside your state and see what they do. Nowadays, platforms like TikTok offer huge reach on short-form videos.

. . .

Important Elements for your Notary Website

As previously mentioned, your Notary business needs a website to get its first clients since you appear more professional and trustworthy whenever potential clients decide to learn more about you. While you need a website to maximize how many clients you have and possibly outperform your competitors, the structure of a well-made Notary website should differ from most sites, such as fashion stores. Fortunately, building a functional Notary website is easy and doesn't require thousands of dollars for web development. Tools like WordPress, Wix.com, GoDaddy.com, and SiteBuilder.com have all you need to build a platform from scratch without a huge budget. Your website should include a homepage, a section about why to choose you, a section about the different services you offer, information about fees and payment methods, a contact form, FAQs, and even a blog if you wish to create blog posts. Additionally, make sure your contact details are prominent, and once you have your first clients - add some testimonials (with customers' prior permission) so that new customers can see how pleased some of your past clients were with your notary services.

7
LOAN SIGNING AGENT MASTERCLASS

<u>The terms "Loan Signing Agent" and "Notary Signing Agent" are used interchangeably in many notary articles, and throughout this chapter, they have the same meaning.</u>

Some information on loan signing agents was already discussed in Chapter 4, but let's go into more detail here and expand on different topics, including the steps of a loan signing and how to grow your loan signing business.

Did you know that ALL loan signing agents are Notary publics, but NOT all Notary publics are loan signing agents? Among the 4.4 million notaries operating in America, it's estimated that as many as 76 % of notary publics are also Loan signing agents. This large proportion of Loan signing agents is due to the high demand for such services by banks, car dealerships, corporate offices, and more. These establishments leverage professionals like us to verify and witness legal and financial documents. If you wish to expand into loan signing or capitalize on the high demand, you should understand the concept thoroughly.

A loan signing agent (LSA) is a Notary public with the required legal and financial certification to guide borrowers through the loan process. To complete these tasks, the Loan Signing Agent must be familiar with loan processes and how they work; otherwise, they won't be able to translate a contract to the customer accurately. Neither Notary publics nor signing agents can give clients legal advice.

<u>A loan signing agent provides a multitude of functions, and these include:</u>

- Providing guidance and identifying documents necessary for the transaction.
- Answering questions that may arise between borrower and lender.

- Initiating communication with professionals involved in the transaction, like a loan officer, title agent, or real estate agent.
- Protecting the lender and borrower's best interests and preventing fraud by noticing red flags in the contract or situation.
- Ensuring that loan packages are executed correctly prevents funds from getting delayed.

While loan signing agents work with multiple corporations - they're often found in the real estate industry since homes, investment properties, and land typically involve taking loans (mortgages). Therefore, you often find professional loan signing agents certifying real-estate-based transactions such as new home loans, refinancing, reverse mortgages, property transfers, and closing contracts.

The Notary's responsibility is to function as an impartial third-party witness and ensure that all parties involved understand and follow the transaction protocol. Their signatures and initials indicate this understanding between the lender and borrower on all related documents.

. . .

What are the key distinctions between a Loan Signing Agent (LSA) and a Notary Public?

At first glance, there is little to no difference when comparing a Loan Signing Agent versus a regular Notary public. This assumption is also compounded by the fact that both agents are available to witness the signing of legal documents. However, in reality, both concepts are different, and here's how:

A **Notary public** is a professional authorized to witness the signing of legal documents, usually affidavits, seeds, licenses, estates, power of attorney, and more. On the other hand, a **loan signing agent** is a certified expert typically focused on the home loan process.

The primary difference between a notary public and an LSA is that the latter can help answer clients' questions about loans, whether for a real estate property, vehicle, home, or business. They can not give legal advice; however, keep in mind. On the other hand, a Notary public isn't equipped with the knowledge to answer such complex and intricate questions; therefore, their duty is only to verify both parties' agreements and signatures on the legal documents. Nevertheless, while both agents perform different tasks, you must become a Notary public before transitioning into a Loan Signing Agent.

Another significant difference between a signing agent and a Notary public is their fees. Essentially, loan signing agents are independent contractors; they decide how much clients pay for their services. This work differs from the Notary public, who are limited by the state limit for Notary public fees. For example, in Illinois, you can only charge $1 for most documents - but in Florida, most are charged at $10 per document. Whereas, as a loan signer, you're free to charge anywhere from $100 to $200+ per assignment. Some additional factors that determine the assignment's cost are the contracting company's budget and whether you're working for an escrow office or lender. Escrow offices typically pay more. Furthermore, as a signing agent, you can charge for courier services, including printing/delivering loan packages to the company or individual.

It, therefore, goes without saying then, that being a loan signing agent is more lucrative. Lucrativeness is a crucial influence to consider when choosing a career path, and if you're contemplating becoming a loan signing agent, the good news is that it pays well. A professional loan signing agent makes between $75 to $200 per appointment or approximately $3000 monthly for part-time agents and $7000 monthly for full-time signing agents. Compensation examples and recent earnings statistics were discussed in more depth in Chapter 4.

Steps to Becoming a Loan Signing Agent (LSA)

Becoming a Loan signing agent is financially rewarding whether you're doing it part-time or full-time. However, to achieve peak financial prosperity, you'll need to follow the right path to success; else, you may struggle with mediocrity.

Here are the required prudent steps:

1. Get Commissioned to be a Notary Public in your state

Begin your journey by getting an active Notary public license (commission). You don't need a college degree or sophisticated education to become a public loan signing agent - but being an active Notary public from your state is the first step. Refer to earlier chapters of this book or your state website to determine the surety bond or any examinations you'll need. However, you can skip this phase if you're already a Notary public.

. . .

2. Take a Loan Signing Training Course

After getting commissioned to be a Notary public in your state, the next step is to be certain of your ability to complete a loan signing confidently. This means that you should have extensive knowledge of where the borrower signs, how to complete the loan signing appointment before your first appointment, and what each document means. Fortunately, this knowledge is easy to acquire since there are a plethora of courses available online to educate you on everything you need to know about loan signing processes. My favorite loan signing agent training course is from nationalnotary.org. **As an example, the complete Florida NSA certification package on National Notary costs $285 and includes background checks, training, examination, and certification. It also includes a top-tier listing for one year on signingagent.com.** On the other hand, basic certification costs $208, and the background check only costs $79.

3. Take an SPW-Compliant Examination

As previously mentioned, no examination or test is mandatory to become a loan signing agent; but without taking an SPW-compliant exam - you won't be eligible for as many jobs, therefore reducing your potential income as an LSA. After completing your course, you will be prepared to take your exam.

· · ·

4. E&O Insurance & Surety Bond

Ensure your surety bond and E&O (errors & omissions) insurance (minimum $25k, $100k is better, though) are in place. You may already have these from when you got your notary commission, but it's worth checking twice in case you need further or extended coverage since now you'll also be working with home loans. Contact your insurance provider or state for more information.

5. Buy your Signing Agent Supplies

Like any other business, some equipment and supplies are essential to fulfilling the trade, and the same applies to your Notary business. Here is a list of everything you'll need - the first four relate to being a notary public, and the items which follow are essential for loan signing agents. So loan signing agents will need everything on the list.

- Notary Stamp (roughly $15)
- Surety Bond (est. $50)
- Notary Journal - state-dependent (roughly $16)
- Thumbprint - state-dependent (roughly $8)
- Messenger Bag - around $30

- Letter Paper - cost depends on the amount
- Legal Paper - cost depends on the amount
- 10 Blue Pens - $2
- E & O Insurance - around $20 a month
- Dual Tray Laser Jet Printer (Ink Jet Printers do not suffice for loan signing documents) - should cost around $300 to $500 - however it can be had for less if second hand.
- Scanner (multi-page) - should be around $200-300

Please note if you only work directly with MLOs (mortgage loan officers), you won't need a printer or scanner, as they will do this for you. However, it'll still be easier for other assignments if you have them yourself.

6. Get Listed on Signing Services to get more Jobs

Signing services exist to help professionals like you to be found by more people. It's similar to how platforms like Fiverr are Upwork connect freelancers to companies and individuals that need their services. Nevertheless, consider registering in as many loan signing databases as you can - like SigningAgent.com, Snap-Docs.com, NotaryRotary.com, NotaryCafe.com, and SigningOrder.com. Ensure to include your name, phone number, email, and social media platforms in as many signing services as possible to get as many jobs as possible. Your loan signing course should show you how to optimize your profile.

7. Begin work as a loan signing agent

After becoming a notary public, passing SPW-compliant examinations, and getting your supplies and insurance, you can proceed to work as a loan signing agent. As well as registering on multiple signing services for jobs, you can communicate and offer your services to escrow offices, loan officers, and real estate agents to begin earning. Convincing these individuals that your services and offerings are worth-while will involve effective communication and sales skills.

How to complete a loan signing:

Before you arrive at your first loan signing, ensure that you first are familiar with all the common closing documents (you'll have learned these in your course/examination), confirm the time/location, read any special instructions, print all necessary docu-ments, and then call the borrower to confirm these things. The following section explains the five most crucial steps to doing your first Loan signing success-fully. These five steps include:

1. Explain the Signing Process

Upon meeting the signer in their home or office, the first step is to introduce yourself and reiterate your importance to the process as a loan signing agent. Inform the borrower that they aren't permitted to mark anywhere on the document except the indicated portions. Also, describe to the borrower how they should sign their name and date the document.

2. Present and Explain the Documents

After briefing your client on the aforementioned best practices, present the documents necessary for the loan and explain each of them. Also, answer whatever questions they may possess - since part of your duty includes rectifying doubts and ensuring your client understands what they are signing.

Here are the most common loan signing documents that you may need to understand and explain:

- Deed of Trust (Mortgage)
- Settlement Statement (HUD-1)
- Notice of Right to Cancel
- Note
- Signature Affidavit and AKA Statement
- Customer Identification Verification

Direct the borrower on where to sign to avoid any mistakes or confusion.

3. Review the Documents

Sometimes, mistakes happen despite how many explanations you provide to your client; that's why it's important to review the documents once they are done. This revision allows you to spot missing signatures, dates, initials, or Notary seal imprints. Once spotted, bring the flaw to your clients and ask for immediate rectification before providing the borrower with a document copy.

4. Contact the Contracting Company

Once your client signs the documents and no error exists on either copy, call your Contracting Company or lender to notify them that the notarization aspect of the loan signing is complete. Afterward, you can forward the loan package to the company via mail or personally to their office.

5. Send your Invoice

After the lender confirms that the documents have been received, send your invoice and await payment for your services.

How to expand your NSA/LSA Business

Business growth goes beyond marketing via social media, your website, or email marketing; most times, your network is all you need to take your Loan signing agent business from failure to success.

Professionalism is one factor that guarantees repeat business with your contracting company since you're a reliable representative of their establishment. Often, your face may be the only contact borrowers have with the lending company, so act professionally, whether at home, in an office, or when signing documents. Answer your calls and emails professionally and remove everything of informality except insisted by the client or contracting company. For example, answer calls or greet with a straightforward "Hello" or "Good morning." Avoid unacceptable "What," "Huh," and "Yeah?". Dress like a business person working in an office and avoid overly casual clothing for appointments. Furthermore, speak professionally and avoid trash-talking, passive aggression, or condescending words, irrespective of the situation.

Networking is currency; it allows other professionals in your industry to recommend you for business whenever they're occupied or unable to handle the task. For this reason, prioritize communication with other signing agents online and in your local communities; it's a reliable way to grow your business and receive recommendations from experienced experts.

Ultimately, becoming a loan signing agent requires multiple certifications, supplies, training, and additional soft skills. Fortunately, these requirements are fairly easy to acquire, and the career path is financially rewarding. And remember, the more you earn, the more you learn!

8

BECOMING A REMOTE ONLINE NOTARY & FURTHER INCOME GENERATING ACTIVITIES

Notaries are state-appointed professionals who witness vital document signings and verify each signer's identity to prevent fraud. These officials exist in different forms, with a popular option being a Remote Online Notary (RON). In fact, statistics show that the adoption of remote online notarizations increased by 547% in 2020, largely due to government protocols surrounding the Covid-19 pandemic and due to **more than 40 states already passing permanent RON legislation.**

A Remote Online Notary is a professional notary public that notarizes documents remotely via electronic signature and audio-visual technologies. They use electronic identity verification and record-keeping technology. These systems ensure that neither the client nor you (the notary) have to leave your home or office to commence business, thereby saving travel and accommodation costs. In other words, as long as the notary uses the recommended Remote Notary technologies that provide full security with encrypted e-signatures and audit logs, notarial acts can be carried out within minutes without needing to meet in a physical location to sign documents. However, this form of notarization can only happen if the state laws permit it, but we'll get to the differences in each state later in this chapter. But first, let's discuss the benefits of becoming a remote online notary.

1. Earning Potential

The typical notary public is constrained to a small portion of their state, unless they have sufficient transportation and marketing means, which are both expensive and time consuming. This restriction results in an average earning potential as the number of clients are fewer. However, a Remote Online Notary (RON) has a larger earning potential since they operate online. Essentially, you can advertise your services via online marketing and attract clients throughout your state. Also, since there's no compulsion to travel or market offline, you won't incur additional unnecessary costs.

• • •

Another huge factor is that state fee limits are often higher for RON transactions - a quick look at the table below from https://www.nationalnotary.org/knowledge-center/about-notaries/notary-fees-by-state demonstrates this. As you can see, the RON fees are often double or up to 5 times that of standard notary public fees. For example, in New Mexico, a verbal oath is charged at $5, but a RON transaction is set at $25.

Image on Next Page (eBook only)

State	Acknowledgments	Jurats	Verbal Oath/ Affirmation	Travel Fees (set by)	RON
Missouri	$5	$5	$5	Not set †	$5*
Montana	$10	$10	$10	IRS	$10 per signature
Nebraska	$5	$2	$2	Dept. of Admin Services	$25
Nevada	$15	$15	$7.50	$15 - $30 per hour †	$25
New Hampshire	$10	$10	$10	$0.20 per mile	$25
New Jersey	$2.50 / $15**	$2.50 / $15**	$2.50 / $15**	N/A	Not set
New Mexico	$5	$5	$5	Not set †	$25
New York	$2	$2	$2	-	N/A
North Carolina	$10	$10	$10	Prohibited	N/A

2. New Learning Opportunities

Working as a Remote Online Notary opens you to new knowledge in fields like Real estate, Law, business, and more. While this is a perk of a Notary public, Remote

Online Notarization presents you with more freedom and time to learn faster and easier.

3. Convenience

Being a Remote Online Notary (RON) means you and your client can perform business without needing to travel or meet face-to-face since you both can connect via a secure platform. In fact, clients will appreciate this factor since they can sign documents in any environment desired and feel relaxed. You'll also save money on travel costs, increasing your profit.

4. Flexible Schedules

Without the necessity of meeting physically to notarize documents, you can easily design your lifestyle with flexibility. Essentially, you'll be able to work from home as a Remote Online Notary with flexible days, hours, and workloads. You can also choose to work full-time or part-time; nevertheless, it allows working in a fulfilling industry while having time to spend on other gratifying activities.

5. Security

Security plays a crucial part in the notary profession since you typically deal with confidential documents.

Fortunately, Remote Online Notarization is the most secure way to Notarize documents because each session is done through secure mediums - with each process being recorded. Additionally, this increased security makes it easy to quickly refer back to the recorded transactions whenever there's a dispute that needs settling.

6. Ease and Speed

Completing your notary business online is hassle-free since the entire process only takes minutes to finish. The average time is as little as 10 minutes depending on the document complexity. Furthermore, a Remote Online Notary (RON) eliminates the hassle of an in-person notary meeting. Instead, you and your clients can complete the business via a smartphone, laptop, or any device with a webcam. All that's needed is to receive their uploaded document, communicate with a via webcam, and commence business.

Ultimately, the benefits of becoming an online notary are plenty and noteworthy, and if you're already a notary public, making the transition would give your career a much-needed boost.

The General Criteria to become a RON

As previously elaborated, Remote Online Notarization (RON) has quickly taken over traditional notary services as it's more convenient, faster, and reliable. However, becoming a Remote Online Notary requires a process alongside you meeting specific requirements. Fortunately, this section will provide what you need to become a legitimate Remote Online Notary in your state.

<u>Here's how:</u>

1. Age Limit and Legal Residence

There's a legal minimum age requirement to becoming a Remote Online Notary; fortunately, the limit is reasonable as interested individuals must be at least 18 years old to operate as notaries. Furthermore, you're required to be a legal resident of your state, the one you wish to begin your RON career, and must have zero felonies before commencing business. Please note that these requirements are the basics, and the application process can change depending on your state.

2. Pay the Fees

There's typically a notary application fee alongside a fee for the exam you will take to become a notary; however, the cost can change depending on your state.

Some additional costs may include essential notary training materials, supplies, and background checks.

3. Fill Out your Application Form

You need to fill out an application form with the Secretary of State as this department provides legal authorization to perform business as a Remote Online Notary.

4. Pass your State's RON Exams

Many states require potential Remote Online Notaries to pass specific exams to test their viability as RONs. This test is offered by the state organizations like the Secretary of State or the Department of State; occasionally, some locations outsource the exam to an outside organization - like Pennsylvania does with Pearson VUE. While the minimum score to pass these exams is dependent on your state of operation, it is often 70%. Nevertheless, devote time to mastering the subject material. You can prepare using any state-approved education resource, like an e-learning notary course. As usual, this differs by state. Virginian RON's require no further training, whereas Ohio notaries would need to pass an exam.

5. Get your Digital Certificate and Software Tools

As previously mentioned, a Remote Online Notary requires specific qualifications and online tools for maximum professionalism and security while doing business. One of these certificates is the IGC Agencies Basic Assurance Unaffiliated digital certificate from IdenTrust, which allows you to operate as an online notary.

To acquire this certificate, you need to visit the IdenTrust official website, start the application process, and submit relevant documents. These documents often include:

- A state-issued ID or Driver's License.
- A debit card or credit card for validating your identity and paying for the certificate.
- Information on your notary commission.

The application process is easy and will take a few minutes to complete, and receiving the digital certificate will take less than 24 hours. Another thing you'll need to get is your notary eSeal. You will need the digital certificate to work on the following platforms. Always check compatibility, as the Identrust certificate is not compatible with Pavaso software, for example.

Some of the most common end-to-end RON platforms which notaries use include:

- PandaDoc
- Notarize.com
- Docusign RON
- Securesigning.com
- Notary.io
- eNotaryLog

There are many more, and you can find reviews of these online to determine which best fits your needs and which is supported by your state. My personal favorite is Notarize.com.

6. Get insurance

You're human, meaning that you're prone to errors in your tasking field. For this reason, we recommend getting E&O insurance with a policy between $25k to $100k to financially protect you if you were to make a mistake. You should also have a surety bond that covers RON, which protects the public. Once you've submitted all documents to the state, you are ready to go!

. . .

States that Allow Remote Online Notarization (RON)

You cannot become a Remote Online Notary in any state that you desire; you first need to confirm whether that location permits such a service. Fortunately, ever since Covid-19, more than 40 states have passed permanent Remote Online Notarization laws, and we can expect more in the future.

<u>Here is a list of 41 states that permit Remote Online Notarization at the time of writing:</u> Alaska, Arizona, Arkansas, Colorado, Florida, Hawaii, Idaho, Illinois, Indiana, Iowa, Kansas, Kentucky, Michigan, Minnesota, Montana, Nevada, New Hampshire, New Jersey, New Mexico, North Dakota, Ohio, Oklahoma, Oregon, Pennsylvania, South Carolina, South Dakota, Tennessee, Texas, Utah, Vermont, Virginia, Washington, West Virginia, Wisconsin, Wyoming.

It's worth noting that the District of Columbia has passed permanent remote notarization laws. However, some other states are still in progress, have a specific date for the law to take effect, or don't permit it.

These include:

- Remote Online Notarization laws in Maine and North Carolina will take effect on July 1, 2023
- Massachusetts and Mississippi have temporary rules on remote notarization
- Vermont's laws on Remote Notarization are in effect, but the rules are pending
- South Carolina hasn't presented any information on whether it is legal or illegal
- Notaries in California cannot perform Remote Online Notarization
- Connecticut and Georgia had temporary Remote Online Notarization permits, which have now expired.

Ultimately, there are currently <u>five states that don't yet allow Remote Online Notarization</u> which include Connecticut, California, Delaware, the District Of Columbia, and Massachusetts. However, some of these states like Delaware don't mention anything that prohibits an individual from using or operating as a Remote Online Notary. These are subject to change at all times and we cannot update the book so frequently, so please use your own wisdom and check online at the time you are reading.

7 Steps To Perform A Remote Online Notarization

. . .

Now that you understand the duties of a Remote Online Notary and how to become a RON, the next phase is understanding how to perform a Remote Online Notarization. Here are the typical seven steps to perform a Remote Online Notarization:

1. Client Contacts the Notary

Proper marketing will result in multiple clients or signers reaching out for a document notarization. This phase begins the process since, where like every other business, commerce begins with the customer's request for your offering or service.

2. Documents Sent to the Notary

Unlike in-person notarization, every aspect of Remote Online Notarization is done over the internet. Therefore, documents need to be delivered to you via a reliable platform, such as one of the six mentioned earlier, like PandaDoc or Notarize.com. Afterward, you can begin the notarization process.

3. Signer Identity Screening

Due to the lack of a physical presence during notarization, rigorous and meticulous signer verification is necessary. The individual is screened according to the requirements of the Notary's state, and the process may include verifying the signer's identification documents online (credential analysis), asking them questions about their personal credit history (Knowledge Based Authentication/KBA), viewing the signer's ID during notarization, or by other trustworthy RON verification methods set by state rules.

4. Clear Audio-visual Communication

To simulate being in the same room as an in-person notarization, the Signer and Notary must communicate via online audio-visual technology. This involves having a microphone and webcam active to maintain proper interaction during the notarization process.

5. Document Signing

Once all notarization requirements are complete, and the notary can verify the signer's identity and authenticity, both parties can proceed to sign the document with the Notary's seal attached to the papers. Since these documents are in digital form and can not be written with a pen or pencil, an electronic signature is required alongside an electronic version of the Notary's seal (eSeal).

. . .

6. Thorough Record Keeping

The Notary's job, whether online or offline, is to witness a document signing, and this involves keeping some records as well. Therefore, as a Remote Online Notary, it's important to record important information in your Notary journal. Furthermore, the record-keeping extends to the audio and video files taken during the notarization process, so they must be preserved and kept as part of prudent record-keeping.

7. Return the Signer's Documents

Once the entire notarization process is complete, proceed to return the completed documents to the signer, which they will download from the platform you used. The whole process isn't time-consuming and often takes less than 20 minutes.

The key difference between RON and e-notarization

While discussing Remote Online Notarization, it's important to distinguish the difference between this concept and e-notarization. Many people have the misconception that Electronic Notarization and

Remote Online Notarization are synonyms describing the same thing; they're not.

E-notarization, also known as Electronic Notarization, involves documents that are notarized in electronic form, where the document signer and Notary sign with an electronic signature. In e-notarization, all aspects of traditional notarization are present, including the need for the notary and signer to meet physically, unlike in Remote Online Notarization. The misconception arises when people assume that since electronic and digital are somewhat synonymous, both concepts must be the same; that is untrue. Essentially, an RON is conducted online without needing an in-person meeting, while e-notarization is required by the state to be present to sign the documents electronically.

Document formatting types for RON vs. RIN vs Traditional vs. e-notarization

Document formatting plays an important role in the corporate sector since it indicates professionalism and also makes your papers easier to process for the reader. Therefore, it makes sense for each type of notarization (Traditional, IPEN, RON, and RIN) to have different formatting requirements for documents.

. . .

Here's an overview of these requirements:

- Traditional notarization requires a document signed with original ink on physical paper.

- In-person electronic notarization (IPEN) uses a PDF, Word file, or any other record, and the document is presented on a computer, tablet, or mobile device.

- Remote online notarization also uses an electronic record as in an in-person e-notarization, but the papers are signed virtually.

- RIN requires a physical document with an original signature written in ink (hence the name remote ink-signed notarization) but may also require that an additional electronic copy be sent to the Notary.

Apostille Services

The word apostille originates from the bible. An Apostille authenticates the signatures and origin of public documents such as court orders, birth certificates, and other documents used by a federal agency or certified by a foreign or American consul. Based on the definition, some people assume an Apostille and a notary public are the same or somewhat similar; this is untrue. Essentially, these two are ideal for different situations; for example, getting a notarization means the document has been certified by a notary public who witnesses and identifies everyone signing the document. On the other hand, an Apostille is an authentication process done by the Secretary of State to verify the signatures of officials that signed a document. Afterward, a certificate will be issued by the Secretary of State attached to the original document as proof of its legitimacy, also making the paper valid in other countries.

While a notary public and an apostille offer different types of services, you can become an agent for the latter and offer apostille services to boost your notary business. Furthermore, this service complements the traditional notary business. Improving your business by offering apostille services is easier if you live near the Secretary of State's office. Since the notary doesn't themself offer apostille services - it's a government service - the notary provides a courier service delivering documents to the state apostille agency, which they can return after processing. These services aren't "notarial" acts, allowing you to determine your service fee with your clients.

Can a Notary do I-9 Form Verification?

The I-9 form is issued by U.S. Citizenship and Immigration Services; it verifies the employment eligibility and identity of employees hired in the U.S. As required by Law, both the employer (or authorized representatives) and employee must fill out the I-9 form alongside the verification of the new hire's identity.

While a notary is legally required to witness a document and verify the signature and authenticity of the signer, there is no "certificate" wording included in the I-9 form, nor is a notary seal required on the form. Therefore notaries can not verify I-9 forms. However, if the employer does want to involve a notary in some regard, they should function as an "authorized representative" and not perform any actual notarization.

Generating Additional Income via Other Mediums

Like many business owners, a notary public has the opportunity to use their position to generate additional income for the Notary business. Some examples include document delivery/printing services, immigration forms, field inspection, and being a wedding officiant. Here are more details on these opportunities:

1. Document Delivery, Printing Services

A notary public deals with documents, which they receive and deliver to clients regularly; you can turn this factor into a side hustle by offering document delivery to companies, agencies, and government bodies. Additionally, you can leverage your high-level laser printer to produce papers for other non-notary-related activities.

2. Immigration Forms

It's not uncommon to encounter clients that need help with immigration paperwork, and while there are strict laws preventing notaries from providing unauthorized legal advice or representing immigrants in court, 14 states allow some level of assistance. The aid includes translating answers on immigration forms, making references to attorneys for legal representation, or securing supporting documents like birth certificates.

<u>The states that support some level of assistance from notaries include:</u>

Arizona Minnesota

California Nevada

Georgia New York

Illinois Oklahoma

Maryland South Carolina

Maine Utah

Michigan Washington

3. Field Inspection

Field inspection is an excellent way for notaries to improve their earnings, as inspectors are the eyes and ears of companies that need tasks completed. Essentially, an inspector operates in three different categories, which include mortgages, insurance, and commercial inspections. Fortunately, becoming a field inspector is hassle-free as corporations require no previous qualifications but a simple background check. Some companies even offer some level of training and explanation of what's expected from you. You can find jobs quickly by searching keywords on Google like "collateral inspection," "business verification," or "freight inspection."

4. Wedding Officiant

Notaries can become ordained ministers to officiate weddings and advertise their services via social media, personal websites, business cards, and brochures. However, before opting for this side hustle, check your state laws as the regulations depend on your location; nevertheless, it's a viable way to expand your business.

Getting in State Clients vs. Out of State Clients

The standard regulation governing notary publics is that they are required to notarize documents within their state. However, if you're curious about whether you can process documents from outside your state, you're not alone!

. . .

The answer depends on the laws your state operates; for example, Montana, Wyoming, and North Dakota are amongst the few states that allow notaries to offer notarization services in other states that support this law. Therefore, suppose a client receives a document in Montana and travels to North Dakota for notarization; you can complete the task without legal complications.

Ultimately, ensure to check your state laws on whether notary publics can notarize out-of-state documents without legal complications; it can help expand your business beyond your state.

9
NOTARY BUSINESS EXPANSION STRATEGIES

There are multiple reasons to diversify your client list and Notary Services, but the two most common include increasing income streams and having a fail-safe option if your primary source of revenue declines. In fact, observations from the American Association of Notaries show that advertised mortgage rates are currently hovering between 6% and 8%, with predictions expecting them to keep creeping up, resulting in a slow-down for many loan signing agents due to the reduction of mortgage applications. This slow-down will produce reduced revenue for notaries that rely on loan signing only. In other words, diversifying is an ideal way to avoid a dip in your income and also expand your business in case the economy continues to slow. Another thing to be said about the future of the industry is that the tendency to perform notarizations online and remotely will surely only increase - so long as the process remains secure and confidential.

<u>Some recommended options for diversity in your notary business include:</u>

1. Document Retrieving

As a notary public, you most likely travel to different locations within your state to notarize documents and transport the papers to their final destination. This skill can function as its standalone side hustle, where you retrieve documents in nearby counties for corporations and government organizations. Places like Secretary of State, national archive locations, or federal clerk offices are common locations that need services like these regularly. On the other hand, you can advertise your new service on your website and signing service profiles to attract customers to your business.

2. Courthouse Couriering, Filing, and Recording Services

Another way to expand your notary business is to provide courthouse gilding of documents and do mortgage recordings. You could also offer daily trips to the courthouse to office managers of small Law offices.

As for marketing, the office of local attorneys specialized in litigation should be your primary target.

3. Real Estate Field Inspections

Your job as a field inspector revolves around sending photos and videos inspecting equipment and properties to clients that need inventory taking. Finding jobs here is relatively easy as companies don't have rigorous requirements and will even train you on what they need. Advertising on your website or communicating with real estate, insurance, and other commercial establishments may be sufficient in getting you a job.

4. Mobile DNA Collecting

DNA collection allows the government or any relevant establishment to collect sensitive and private information. Therefore, as a mobile DNA collector, your job is to collect and deliver the details to the organization, like how you would deliver signed documents as a Mobile Notary Public. The financial compensation associated with the job ranges between $25 to $90 per session, serving as a profitable side hustle for your notary business.

. . .

On the topic of notary business expansion, closing agents and escrow offices are two common sources of patronage, as both departments revolve around heavy paperwork. Essentially, a closing agent, also known as a settlement agent, ensures that all parties involved receive documents during a mortgage loan closing. Furthermore, these agents provide escrow instructions to other parties, like estate agents, in order to receive commissions and fees.

On the other hand, Escrow offices, also referred to as escrow companies, are neutral third parties that collect the required documents and funds needed in the closing process. The document includes the loan papers, signed deeds, and initial earnest money check.

However, suppose you had to choose between working for a closing agent or escrow office; which pays better? Based on my data and experience, earnings from escrow offices are generally higher, as illustrated in Chapter 2.

10

PERMIT RENEWALS, FAQS, TAKING PAYMENTS & MORE

As you can imagine, certificates expire, and your notary public permit typically expires within four years beginning on the date the notary commission was issued by the government. Renewing this document is crucial since failing to restart the expiring date is regarded as a class C misdemeanor by the law, which would negatively impact your business. Fortunately, this section is dedicated to guiding you through the notary public certificate renewal process, making it as straightforward as possible.

Read on!

Notary Public Certificate Renewal Process

It's worth noting that the Notary Public Certificate renewal process, requirements, and costs, differ from state to state; nevertheless, below are the general processes shared by most locations.

These are:

1. Finish any testing or training required by your state
2. Complete a Notary application form
3. Purchase and file your bond and oath
4. Receive your commission
5. Order your Notary supplies and seal
6. Continue your notary duties

Avoid waiting for your notary public certificate to expire before renewing the document, as it often becomes a legal issue after 90 days of expiration. We recommend beginning the renewal process at least six months before your current commission expires. If you're new to renewing your Notary Public commission, you need all the necessary information to avoid mistakes that may be detrimental to your notary business.

. . .

For this reason, here are some common questions answered about the notary public certificate renewal process:

What happens once my notary commission expires?

Once your notary certificate exceeds four years, the state will no longer recognize you as a notary public, meaning you can not notarize documents anymore. Furthermore, any documents notarized with your expired documents will be invalid and will result in a class C misdemeanor.

Must I take tests and courses to renew?

It depends on your state. Some locations have education and tests that are mandatory for renewing your Notary documents. On the other hand, some states don't require any examination except if you take too long to renew your notary commission.

How long will the renewal process take?

The time needed to renew your notary public license varies from state to state, as some locations complete the activity within a few days or weeks. On the other hand, some states can take up to six months due to factors like application volume, agency staff levels, budget cuts, and the number of steps needed to renew the commission.

How much does it cost?

The cost to renew your notary public license depends on your state.

What notary equipment is necessary?

Upon renewing your Notary license, you will need a new notary seal and Notary journal; however, you can continue using your previous journal in some cases, especially if the time between the commission expiry and renewal is negligible.

Is a bond or insurance necessary?

A surety bond and E&O insurance protects you and your clients from any mistake or misconduct caused during notarization, and this protection comes when paying damages up to the bond amount. It's worth noting that some states require you to purchase a surety bond alongside your new commission.

Tips to Ensure Early & Prompt Payments

Understanding how to get paid on time is crucial to running your notary business since some companies and individuals will sometimes delay your payments or mess you around. Timely payments allow you to notarize documents as efficiently as possible since you can cover costs for paper, transportation, and more.

1. Present Your Invoices

One effective strategy for getting paid on time is sending your client an invoice for each assignment regardless of whether they need an invoice. Even if the customer requests that you complete an assignment form, you should still include your invoice. You can use standard graphic design software to create your notary public invoice and ensure each one has a unique number for identification. Additionally, your invoice must contain all previously-discussed fees, state taxes, due dates, payment terms, bank details, description of service rendered, and reference to contracts and agreements, etc.

Once the notarization is done, send the invoice to your client alongside a self-addressed envelope to facilitate the payment process.

2. Monitor Your Receivables

Monitor your receivables and check the expiry dates of payments, as it allows you to follow up on accounts that become delinquent. You can track outstanding invoices by creating a special folder named "Unpaid Invoices." Ensure to follow up on these companies/individuals that haven't paid, as hoping the payment will arrive will only delay your well-earned money. Once they fulfill their side of the contract, move their invoice from the "Unpaid Invoice" folder to one with paid clients.

3. Keep a Short Collection Cycle

As soon as a pending payment exceeds its due date, begin the collection process and maintain a well-managed, short collection cycle. This recommendation is based on statistics which illustrate collectors secure more funds with a shorter debt recovery process.

4. Remain Professional

Irrespective of the situation or relationship you have with the debtor, ensure your communication is polite, professional, respectful, and reasonable. In other words, don't raise your voice, swear, or make nasty comments. While your anger and frustration are justified, it doesn't grant you permission to threaten or harass anyone; some states even make this action illegal, so remain calm.

. . .

5. Prepare Yourself

Before picking up the phone to contact the individual or company about their outstanding payment, first, prepare yourself for the interaction. In other words, review the documents, agreements, and other relevant elements to refresh your memory and give you a stronger argument during the interaction. Also, have the papers and related documents ready for quick reference whenever needed.

6. Stay Focused

It's not uncommon for debtors to steer conversations in a different direction, distracting you from your original topic. Debtors often use long stories or excuses to stall and waste time; in this case, you simply return to the original discussion, which is obtaining a commitment to pay, like a date to expect or come pick up the check.

7. End on a Resolution

Avoid ending the conversation with open-ended statements like "I'll see what I can do," "I'll get back to you this week," or "I'll give you a call soon ." Instead, the conversation should end with an agreement to pay, a negotiated settlement, a date to receive payments, and which medium of the transaction (check or bank transfer). Ending the conversation without specifying this factor will only delay the payment again.

8. Keep Records

Ensure to keep detailed records of your efforts to collect payment from the company or individual since these will help your case if it goes to court. Therefore, keep a photocopy of letters, voice calls, and emails, alongside their dates.

9. Prevent Future Delays

Avoid taking new signings for a company or individual that still owes you money as they're less likely to pay for the new assignment if the previous one is unpaid. Therefore, prevent additional damage by refusing assignments until they pay up.

That brings us to the end of the main content.

CONCLUSION

Congratulations, you've made it to the end of this book, guiding you through your Notary Public and Loan Signing Agent journey. If you reflect on what we covered throughout, you'll discover that building a successful Notary business, whether as a side hustle or full-time career path isn't all that complicated; all you need is some drive and the right information. Business experts like Tim Ferris and Robert Kiyosaki identify branding and marketing as a crucial part of any new business as it plays a crucial role in bringing your first generation of customers. Fortunately, creating awareness for your notary business isn't challenging, especially when you have the internet at your fingertips. On the other hand, you can also join local organizations to network and connect with individuals that may require your services or have colleagues that need assistance. Online directories also put you on a catalog of other notaries, allowing people to find your profile on a platform they trust.

The profit potential for a notary or loan signing agent business is notable, and the expected monthly earnings can be in excess of $6000, depending on your state and workload. Furthermore, different types of notaries exist, with the most common types being Loan Signing Agents and Remote Online Notaries; the former specializing in notarizing loan documents, ensuring that the signer understands the documents and that their identity is verified before placing their signature in the designated box. The latter, a Remote Online Notary, can be a Loan Signing Agent or any other type of Notary, but the primary differentiator is the medium of notarization. In effect, a Remote Online Notary public notarizes documents via a reliable platform over the internet, thereby saving you and your client time and money.

Keep in mind that your notary commission isn't indefinite as it often expires within four years; furthermore, failure to renew the license results in a class C misdemeanor, which can negatively affect your record. Therefore, we recommend beginning the certificate renewal process six months before expiration since the time needed to restart your permission can take a few weeks to several months. Nevertheless, operating as a notary public is an excellent way to generate an income, whether as a side hustle or full-time career path. However, clients can delay payments sometimes, and this hesitance is detrimental since you'd rather have a constant stream of income. Stay on top of this with our tips from the previous chapter.

If you take away only one piece of information from this book, it should be that being a loan signing agent is a relatively untapped profession with uncapped earnings. While you will struggle at times, the payoff is worthwhile due to the high income and fulfilling, important work to society.

If you enjoyed reading this book and learning all there is to know about becoming a notary public and LSA, please share the book with your friends or colleagues and leave a positive five-star review. It means a lot knowing that you found this information helpful and encourages us to publish more invaluable resources for your consumption.

Thank you for reading!

Yours,   Fred   Becker
(FredBeckerNotary@Protonmail.com)